OM
Our Cosmic Connection

SOME COMMENTS...

"I was impressed that the author has taken of OM... I sincerely congratulate the author for her great attempt on OM. It is the need of the hour."

Swami Jitatmanandji, Rajkot

"Different aspects of OM are extolled in different places. The need to consolidate scattered descriptions and ideas into a coherent whole and to present it to the common man in a cogent manner is fulfilled by Meera's timely book "*OM– Our Cosmic Connection.*" Timely, because we are today living in a troubled and divided world. Any idea, action, or book that emphasizes our cosmic connection contributes to bringing about peace and harmony among people and communities– a pressing need in today's world."

"The book is a valuable addition to the Hindu theological literature. It serves to bring together varied aspects of OM scattered through the scriptures in one volume, relating the wisdom of the ages with the discoveries of modern science. The narrative is simple and smooth, while it provides guidence to the more curious reader to the scriptural roots."

Prof. Rajendra K. Arora, Florida State University, Florida

'OM is everything and all pervading. The authoress examines it from different perceptions like sound, space, air, energy, water, earth, time (or timelessness), revelation and singularity, and develops the idea in classified chapters. Om is present everywhere in the universe (or universes); but not necessarily as sound. It may be in other form of energy like light or heat or electricity. It is the cosmic radiation and energy. It is present in the microcosm as well as in the macrocosm.

It is a tough assignment to see that the ideas of spirituality match with those of science. The authoress, Mrs. Meera Prakash deserves to be congratulated for endeavouring to establish it is many cases. In addition she has also attempted a more broad-based reconciliation of the basic concepts of different religions and schools of philosophy.

The lucid style and the cogency of presentation add to the flavour and depth of thoughts. Cardinal truths, stated in cryptic words are found all over the text."

Dr. S. Sundaram (Retd), Ramakrishna Mission,
Vivekanand College, Chennai

OM
Our Cosmic Connection

Meera Prakash

SHIPRA

Price : ₹ 495 US$ 25

ISBN: 978-81-7541-520-1

First Published in India in 2011

OM : Our Cosmic Connection

Published by:

SHIPRA PUBLICATIONS

LG 18-19, Pankaj Central Market,
I.P. Ext., Patparganj, Delhi-110092
Ph. 91-11-22235152, 22236152

Br. Off: 4617/18, Ansari Road, Daryaganj,
Delhi-110002; Ph. 65946453, 9810522367
Email: info@shiprapublications.com
www.shiprapublications.com

To my daughter
Pavithra
who took pride in my work and
encouraged me to persevere in
my search for
OM

Contents

Author's note

The reason for this book is two-fold: To extol the virtues of OM as a symbol of humanity and to connect it to scientific theories about the start of the universe – the why and how of it. You may ask, another book trying to connect ancient scriptures to modern scientific revelations? Yes. However, my attempt has been to only correlate the common aspects to science from the point of view of laity, and as a tool to be in harmony with the universe. In my defence I have this to say. I have come across much information through books and audio-visual means about the formation of the universe – both in religious and scientific terms. It is patent that at one point we stumble about in darkness, unable to fathom that infinite power before the start of the universe. While science is totally mystified, religion talks in symbols of the mystic elements of the universe. Trying to imbibe knowledge of the Creative Force of the universe, and the universe is like trying to fill a pot with the waters of the ocean. My journey has been like that of Narada who asked sage Sanatkumara to teach him about that infinite Source. The sage said: "Tell me what you know and then I will teach you whatever is beyond that." When Narada proudly proclaimed all that he knew (which was considerable considering it was sage Narada), sage Sanatkumara blew it off saying: "All that you know is just the name (words). Meditate on the name as Brahman." (Chandogya Upanishad VII – 23.1) While my knowledge is definitely nowhere near that of sage Narada, I did feel that exploring the Name, the Word, would reveal an ounce of the knowledge of the universe.

Of all the religious symbols, the mystic symbol **OM** both baffles and tantalizes one with secrets of that moment before creation. Since it permeates and girdles the entire universe and is within every atom and every human being and vibrates 24 hours a day, it seemed to me the most apt phenomenon to explore. While the Vedas and their Upanishads and the Puranas give glimpses of it, and extol one aspect of it or the other in great detail, I have not found any single source that deals with all aspects of OM.

It is my intent to show through this book that OM represents all aspects of the known and unknown universe, and that it is the connecting link between what is known and unknown. It is a symbol of peace and its peace can be harnessed and enjoyed. OM is a non-personal symbol, in that, it is not necessarily a religious symbol. It is more a cosmic symbol and benefits anyone who will acknowledge it. The conclusions I have drawn about the presence of OM in every aspect of the universe are my individual view points based on what scriptures say and what science is pretty much reiterating today. Everything in the universe is moved by vibration and vibration is nothing but OM.

The Mandukya Upanishad says:

"OM, which is the imperishable Brahman, is the universe."

Mundaka Upanishad further elucidates:

> "Within the lotus of the heart, Brahman dwells, where like the spokes of a wheel in its hub, the nerves meet...Meditate on Him as OM. Easily mayest thou cross the sea of darkness."

The Katha Upanishad sheds further light:

> "The Supreme Brahman is the size of a thumb and dwells in the heart of the beings."

Thus OM is within every being and vibrates within us. Every breath we inhale and exhale is OM, and it runs through our blood and heart and *nadis* (chords or pulse points), which we can hear when we close our ears with our palms, which we have been used to hearing in the womb (and can still hear submerged under water). It is the symbol of the state of being. When we consciously acknowledge it and meditate on it, it pervades our spirits and creates harmony. It is a small symbol and even smaller to recite, but with deep results.

Invocation

OM, the Pranava shabda that is Lord Ganesha
OM, the spark off Lord Shiva's third eye
OM, the universe that is Lord Kartikeya
OM, the creation that Lord Brahma creates
OM, the universe that Lord Vishnu preserves
OM, the sound Goddess Saraswati inhabits
OM, the energy Goddess Shakti initiates
OM, the manifest that is Goddess Lakshmi
OM, I bow to That Absolute Truth.

OM – Some Commentaries

FROM SRI SHANKARACHARYA DISCOURSES

The Mundaka Upanishad talks about 'Akshara Brahman'. The *Akshara* or the syllable 'OM' plays the chief role. This Upanishad says that the arrow of the *Atma* (soul) should be shot from the bow of Omkaara at the target Brahman without wavering so that they (arrow and target) are conjoined and become one.

The Maandukya Upanishad shows the way to transcend the three stages of *Jagrati* (wakeful-ness), *swapna* (dream) and *Sushupti* (sleep) and reach the Turiya or the fourth stage. It says it is possible to reach the final stage in one leap by means of worshipping Omkaara.

This establishes the doctrine, by using the four parts of Pranava (OM), that *Jeevatma* (soul) and *Paramatma* (Superior Soul) are the same. It is also famous for describing as 'Sivan Advaitam' (beautiful and without a second) the fourth and final stage to which finally all creation shrinks.

The Upanishad says "all the Vedas together talk of a single Being." (Kathopanishad 2.15) What is that 'Being'? Vedic consensus is that the 'Being' is that which is represented symbolically by the sound 'AUM'.

(Excerpted from Swami Chinmayananda "Mantra and Japa – Gayatri Meditation and Life".)

Of all the mantras, the most powerful and the significant one is the single syllabled incantation called the Pranava. This is the OM. The available literature on the significance of the Vedic Mantra is almost voluminous. Nowhere in the world can we meet with a more sacred symbol that has got such a vast amount of significance.

From the Vedic times until the present day the word 'OM' has been taken as a symbol and as an aid to meditation by the spiritual aspirants. It is accepted both as one with Brahman and as the medium connecting man and God.

There's a verse in the Vedas:

"Prajapati vai idam agra asit
Tasya vak dvitiya asit
Vag vai Paraman Brahma"

Meaning: "In the beginning was Prajapati, the Brahman with whom was the Word
And the Word was verily the Supreme Brahman."

This sphota has its symbol in the word OM. The sound OM is also called 'Pranava', meaning that it is something that pervades life, or runs through *prana* or breath.

...OM thus represents the entire manifested world and the unmanifested, and also that which is beyond, both the manifest and the unmanifest - the Brahman, which is the changeless substratum for the changing objects of the world of experience.

To every mantra 'OM', the Pranava is added on. And without OM, no sacred chant has its power. Just as a living body has no vitality when the life-giving breath is not flowing through its veins, so too, a mantra has no life in it without the addition of pranava.

FROM THE GOSPEL OF SRI RAMAKRISHNA

The sound OM is Brahman. The rishis and sages practiced austerity to realize the Sound Brahman. After attaining perfection one hears the sound of this eternal Word rising spontaneously from the navel. "What will you gain," some sages ask, "by merely hearing this sound?" You hear the roar of the ocean from a distance. By following the roar, you can reach the ocean. As long as there is a roar, there must also be an ocean. By following the trail of OM you attain Brahman, of which the *Word is the symbol.* That Brahman has been described by the Vedas as the ultimate goal.

...The Sändhya merges in Gayatri, the Gayatri in OM, and OM in Samadhi. It is like the sound of a bell: t-a-m. The yogi, by following the trail of the sound OM, gradually merges himself in the Supreme Brahman.

THE MEANING OF OM
(According to Swami Vivekananda)

This eternal Sphota, the essential eternal material of all ideas or names, is the power through which the Lord creates the universe: nay, the Lord first becomes conditioned as the Sphota, and then evolves Himself out as the yet more concrete sensible universe. This Sphota has one word as its only possible symbol, and this is OM. And as by no possible means of analysis can we separate the word from the idea, this OM and the eternal Sphota are inseparable, and therefore, it is out of this holiest of all holy words, the mother of all names and forms, the eternal OM, that the whole universe may be supposed to have been created. ...OM is the only possible symbol which covers the whole ground...it is not any definite word in its fully formed state. That is to say, if all the peculiarities which distinguish one word from another be removed, then what remains will be the Sphota; therefore, this Sphota is called the Nada-Brahma, the Sound Brahman, because the three letter AUM, pronounced in combination as OM may well be the generalized symbol of all possible sounds. If properly pronounced, this OM will represent the whole phenomenon of sound production, and no other word can do this; and this, therefore, is the fittest symbol of the Sphota, which is the real meaning of OM.

WHAT SCRIPTURES SAY ABOUT OM

Ethadyevakshram Brahma ethadyevakshram param
Ethadyevakshram gyatva yo yadichati tasya tat

"It is OM. It is indeed Brahman. It is the greatest.
Realizing this OM, whatever one desires, that one gets."

(The second line implies that if one desires the Hiranyagarbha or the manifested universe, then one attains that, and if one desires the Supreme Brahman, one attains that.) (Katha Upanishad I.2.16)

Na jayate mriyate va vipashchin
Nayam kutashchinna babhuva kashchita
Ajo nityaha shashvatoyam purano
Na hanyate hanyamane sharire

"This intelligent Self (OM) is neither born, nor does It die.

It does not originate from anything (It is beyond cause and effect).

It is birthless, eternal and imperishable.

It does not die even when the body perishes."

(Katha Upanishad: I.2.18)

Omityetad Aksharamidam sarvam tasyopavyakhyanam
Bhutam bhavadbhavishyaditi sarvam Onkara eva
Yacchanyam trikaalaatitam tadyonkara eva

"The syllable OM is the entire universe. Its explanation is thus:

The past, present and future are all verily OM indeed.

And whatever exists beyond this three division of time, that also is OM." (Mandukya Upanishad 1)

Giraam asmi ekam aksharam

"Among words, I am the one syllable OM."

(Bhagwad Gita: 10.25)

"OM is the bow, the individual being is the arrow and Brahman is the target. With a tranquil heart, take aim, and become one with Him." (Mundaka Upanishad: II.2.4)

"Satyakama, OM is both immanent and transcendent (personal and impersonal).

Meditating upon it can yield either the personal or the impersonal." (Prasna Upanshad: V.2)

Na tatra suryo bhanti na Chandra tarakam, Nema vidyuto kuto ayam agnihi

Tameva bhantam anubhati sarvam, Tasya bhasa sarvamidam vibhati

"There the sun does not shine, nor the moon and the stars
Nor is there a flash of lightning, what to say of Agni (fire)
Because of Him (Brahman) shining, everything shines
Through His effulgence, everything is illuminated."

(Katha Upanishad: II.2.15)

Angushtta matraha Purushontaratma
Sada jananaam hridaye sannivishtaha

"The size of a thumb is the Purusha, the indwelling Self
He is ever seated in the hearts of beings."

(Katha Upanishad: II.3.17)

SPECIAL COMMENTARY

Dr. S. Sundaram*

We find the living and the non-living in our surroundings. Man differs from animals essentially in that he has the power to discriminate, say, between good and evil, right and wrong and truth and falsehood. Animal are incapable of rational thinking. Man, however is equipped for this exercise. He has always been trying to find out the meaning and purpose of life; the logic that links the creator, creation and the created. Though he remains on top of the ladder of evolution, often his thinking is clouded. He tries to understand science, discover truth and progress towards this goal. There are many obstacles. Pursuing science, man comes across its limitations and pushes on to the domain of spirituality.

A rich variety of man's experiences in the spiritual realms has been recorded in the Upanishads. They are the repository of experiences and speculations of many rishis coverring a millennium or more. We find varied conceptions of man, the Universe and the reality in these texts. They accept and affirm the diversity of the phenomenal world and yet declare that it is all Brahman, the Absolute. "From Brahman the universe arose and to Him it will return" (Mu. U.1.1.7; Tai, U III.1). The doctrine that Brahman the ultimate cause does not undergo any change, though it may appear to have changed into the universe is taught in the Upanishads (Chan. U. VI. 1.4.6). There is also another view according to which the effect is the result of a change in the cause. Thus Brahman desired to be many, created the three elements, viz, fire, water and earth in their subtle forms and entered into them and by their combination all other things have been found (Chan. VI. 23.4). According to Brihadaranyaka Upanishad (II 4.5), the goal of life is identity with Brahman and it can be reached in this very life as it is the rediscovery of man of what he already is.

---

* *Retd. Reader, Department of Chemistry, Ramakrishna Mission, Vivekananda College, Chennai*

The means of attaining the goal, has also been discussed. Hearing about the Truth, reflection on it and mediation are enjoined by many earlier Upanishads, while a synthesis of activity and meditation is taught by the later ones. Various means have been recommended by our ancestors for leading us to our destination. An intelligent man must merge his speech (all organs) in the mind, the mind in the intellect, the intellect in cosmic intelligence and that again the placid self (Ka. U. III, 7-8.13).

Concentration with the help of Om is portrayed in Mundakopanishad (II.2.3-4). "Taking the great weapon, the bow, fix the arrow, sharpened by meditation. Drawing it within the mind rapt in the Imutable, pierce the target, that very Immutable." Om is the bow, the soul is the arrow and Brahman is its target. One must pierce it with concentration of mind and become like the arrow, one with it.

Om is a symbol but it reveals the graded existences by making us responsive to the cosmic vibrations. And Om itself is a vibration. It is the name and symbol of Brahman–*Om lti Brahma* (Tai. U. 1-8; Ka. U. l. 2.16) Searching for the essences of things we reach brahman. Also we are to deduce everything from that Om, for everything is from Om and everything is penetrated through and through by Om. Om is everything (Cha. U. II.23.3; *Mā*. U.l). Could a mere-repetitive utterence of Om take us to *Brahman*? Sage vasishta declares in *Yoga Vāsishta;* "The sage Uddālaka then sat down in the lotus posture with his eyes half-closed in medidation. He uttered the holy world *Om* which bestows the highest state." (Yoga Vasishta, 26).

The three letters *a, u* and *m,* constituting the *Pranava* or *Aum (Om)* represent the three gunas– sattva, rajas and tamas; these are embodied in Vishnu, Brahma and Siva; *Om* is but a subtle form of the sacred formula, *hamsah,* also called *ajapa-mantra,* which is the carrier (*vahana*) of Brahma, the creator in as much as hamsah means 'the breath of life'. *Ham* is inspired breath *Sah* is that which is expired. The aspirant has to learn that the *pranava* contains within itself, besides the aforesaid three letters, *bindu* (point), naada (sound), *sakti* (power) and *santa* (quiescence). The *pranava* is the most sacred and the most ancient *bijakshara.*

The Upanishads refer to *Om* as the mystic syllable *par* excellence. It is attractive because its repetition, even if it were to be monotonous, has the effect of bringing about concentration, if not cessation of thought. Therefore it is often regarded as the subject of meditation, the most natural expression for God (Isvara). It has a role to play in the yogic prescription "comtemplate, concentrate and conquer!".

The approach and views of science are not always the same as those of spirituality. For example, science holds that man evolved from monkey. But the fact remains that a sage can produce an ape and the reverse is not possible. According to ancient scriptures, Rishi Kasyapa begot most of the other species!

Om, this single-syllabled sacred chant is the most powerful of all *mantras* and it invariably preceeds all of them. This *sphota,* is called the *Naada Brahman.*The totality of existence is *pranava* and so there is no wonder, it permeates through the entire gamut of human knowledge and more, be it quantum mechanics or astrophysics, quarks or charms, origin of universe or astronomy, relativity or randomness (entropy), poetry or prose, the Absolute or the Omnipotent. There is unity in diversity and that unity is *Om.*

"I am *Om* in all Vedas" declared Lord Sri Krishna in Bhagavad Gita (VII. B). Volumes and volumes have been written on the various aspects of *Om.* For example, scholars like Appayya Dikshita have considered 256 matras of *Om.* Others have dealt with it as a mantra, consisting of eight limbs, *A, U, M,* Ardhamatra, Naada, Bindu, Kala and Sakthi and so on.

Man cannot get all knowledge from science alone. A domain of spirutuality lies ahead to be explored and a constant endeavour to reach the ultimate goal through this zone is essential. This book attempts to bridge this gap in a limited stretch and as such could be deemed to be a significant contribution and would help aspirants.

It is evident that a good amount of background work and research has gone into the preparation of this book. I am sure readers would be immensely benefited by this scholarly and multifaceted work.

Prof. Rajendra K. Arora*

The symbol ॐ, read OM or AUM, is recognized in the Hindu scriptures, including the Vedas, their Upanishads, the Puranas and the Bhagavad Gita, as their most sacred word. It is the symbol of the eternal Sphota – the indescribable material of all concepts and power through which God created the Universe. Commonly understood as a sound or a mantra, OM is the true symbol of God. It is identified in the scriptures with numerous attributes of life and matter, of the known and the unknown, of the manifest and be unmanifest.

Citing the authority of Katha Upanishad, OM is identified with Brahman and with the intelligent Self. The Mandukya Upanishad identifies OM with the entire universe, and so on.

The three components that together make the sound of ॐ (A-U-M) remember the holy trinity: Brahma (the Creator), Vishnu (the Preserver) and Shiva (the Destroyer). This sound was generated when the universe came into being (the Big Bang). This is the echo that constantly sounds within us – the resonance that we hear when we cover our ears with the palms of our hands or when we hold a conch shell to the ear. It is the sound of the universe; it is the voice of silence.

The vibrations associated with sounding of the word OM signify not only the compressions and rarefactions that they generate in the air, but all vibrations that together make up the cosmic energy. These vibrations include photons and electromagnetic waves in the ether that need no material medium for their travel, the pulsations of matter and gyrations of electrons around atomic nuclei. OM encompasses all patterns and rhythms, including the notes of music, the chirping of birds, the ultrasound by which bats perceive objects, the beating heart, the sensory waves of our nervous system, the dance of neurons within the brain, the tidal waves in the ocean, the orbiting of planets round the Sun and of the Moon round the Earth.

---

* Professor of Electrical and Computer Engineering, Florida A & M University and Florida State University, College of Engineering, Tallahassee, Florida

Om is unbounded space with all its visible and dark matter, it is the microcosm of the macrocosm, it signifies all existence with its cause-effect relationships, consciousness, activity and perception. It is the air that we breathe, it is the vital force *Prana,* it is the thinking mind.

OM is energy that manifests itself in motion (kinetic energy) or as electric, magnetic, chemical, nuclear or light energy. Indeed, all matter is energy in a concentrated form, revealed in atomic reactions or explosions and in stellar emissions. OM includes also subtler forms of energy such as the endless potential energy in man. All forces of action and reaction as well as forces of good and evil are embodied in OM. This symbol of the eternal Sphota is the essence of Nature that leads to knowledge and wisdom through the media of existence, sound, space, air, energy, water, earth, mind, senses, karma, austerity and revelation.

Meera leads the reader through a detailed discussion of the foregoing aspects, and more, eventually to the vital questions of birth, death, attainment of happiness, spirituality and realization of the Self. Sadhana, through the practice of yoga and meditation, is an aspect of OM. Concentration on OM renders prayer efficacious.

Amidst all the seeming diversity in Nature, there is an underlying unity. You close the book with a connected vision of the Universe in which contradictions exist only that they may be annihilated through realization of the ultimate Singularity – OM.

Introduction

OM is the most natural sound in the universe. The thought, touch and sound of OM vibrates through every being, every animate and inanimate principle, the entire universe, 24 hours a day. It is the precursor of the universe. Yet, theologians and cosmologists have been hard put to describe it in absolute terms. We get whiffs of it here and there. Sages and Rishis have described it in the Vedas and Upanishads sometimes as space, sometimes as water, sometimes as a golden embryo, as Pure Self, Brahman etc. Cosmologists have described it as mass of energy concentrated in a single point, a cosmic egg, which caused the Big Bang, before space and time came into existence. They have also stated that it is impossible to describe what is after all infinite and can only be speculated upon.

Aristotle pondered this question deeply and came to the conclusion that there are four causes for the state of being:

a) What makes it,
b) What it is made of,
c) What caused its shape,
d) What is the reason for it,

He called it the responsible cause, the material cause, the formal cause and the final cause.

The most important mantra of the Vedic religion – The Gayatri Mantra, invokes the Absolute as the light that illuminates the four worlds:

a) Space – Subtle or psychical - i.e. the responsible cause
b) Time – Physical - i.e. the material cause
c) Causal – Potential, formal - i.e. the formal cause
d) Transcendental – the meta-physical cause for it – i.e., the final cause

This sameness of thought is easy to understand, for OM is a thought. Speculation about the universe and beyond proceeds in similar patterns. But OM is also beyond thought. It can be defined, and yet, it is beyond identification. So, what is OM?

No one can ever know what exactly OM is and what all it encompasses. That it encompasses everything known and unknown *is a given*. OM is many things, many concepts, and all the elements in the universe. In fact, OM is the universe. OM is the origin sound of the universe. But when you say sound, you limit its function to that of only sound. OM is more than just sound. OM is the starting point of the universe. OM is the mysterious first, original source from which sound, space and time emerged. OM is the beginning, the end and the entire functioning of the universe.

Before OM rent the universe, there was no sound, no light coming out of that void. Whatever it was was self-contained. It was soundless, incomprehensible, inconceivable and indescribable. Even today, after the manifestation of the universe from that dense point of energy (which was pitch black, which has been described in Genesis as 'Black Fire') and soundlessness, that self-contained sphere remains nameless and untraceable and as incomprehensible as ever. Why? The Shiva Purana gives a glimpse as to why?

"At first there was nothing. The planets, stars, sun etc. were not there and everywhere was nothing but darkness. The moon, fire, water, morning, night, abstract and reality – nothing was there. In this confusing emptiness, there was only 'SattBrahma', that is 'Satt' or 'that which is', and 'Brahma' the 'self-contained'. This 'Satt' is beyond place, voice and five elements, name and guise. It is without illumination and has no body, without any dual qualities. It has neither a beginning nor an end. It is omnipotent, omnipresent and omniscient."

Given such a description, it is hardly surprising that our concept of that time, before creation, always falls short of the Absolute Truth. However, science and scriptures give clues to it, and it is in the nature of thinking beings to forever try to solve that mystery. Even if we cannot know its entire composition, quality and true essence, we can conceive what all it can be in the form of OM, through OM. It is the most comprehensive, non-credal spiritual sound and symbol of the universe.

OM, the origin sound of the universe, the quintessence of God may be difficult to understand in pure, sublime terms, but in human terms, we can categorize it under space, time, light, energy, air, sound, earth, water, enlightenment and singularity. OM, also known as AUM has meters to it. A, 'Akara' is the earth. U, 'Ukara' the heavens and space. M, 'Makara' is air and enlightenment. 'Ardhamatra' (half curve) is naada or sound. 'Bindu' (dot) is atom, energy, and elements, and 'Kaala' (curve under dot) is time. Akara, ukara, makara, ardhamatra, naada, bindu and kaala all keep beat and mark time.

The Mandukya Upanishad describes this AUM as the three aspects of the Self. 'A' the first aspect is the universal person. The heavens are his eyes, the air his breath, the fire his heart, the water his belly, the earth his feet, the space his body. Associated with these are the five organs of sense, five organs of action, five functions of the breath, plus mind, ego and intellect and heart. 'U' the second aspect is the mental nature reflected in the light of the collective universal person. 'M' the third aspect is the universal person in dreamless sleep –called Prajna. Beyond these, is OM. This is Self beyond all comprehension, One without a second.

However as we look at it, OM seems to encompass all aspects of the known universe, and the unknown beyond.

The Story of Lord Kartikeya

The universe started out from a pinpoint of energy, from a spark. 'Onkara dhwani' (sound of Om), rent the cosmos. Scientists call it the Big Bang. This phenomenal event is described through the story of Lord Kartikeya's birth.

The Devas (angels) needed the son of God to help them win the war against the demons. They prayed to Lord Shiva to end their troubles by bestowing his son upon them. Lord Shiva was pleased with their prayers and gathered all his energy (Shakti) unto himself. Then from the third eye on his forehead (the eye of knowledge), sparks flew and landed on the world. The spark was so hot that even Agni Deva (fire) himself could not touch it. Since it was heating up the universe, Agni picked it up and ran to submerge it in the cooling waters of the Ganges flowing from Lord Shiva's matted locks. The Ganges started swirling with heat and threw it out on the shara grass. There it split into six and six beautiful babies took form. Six celestial nymphs (Kirtikas) came to earth to take care of the infants. Agni, Ganges and the Kirtikas, all claimed the infants. But Lord Shiva said that since the infants were born of pure energy, only Shakti (Parvati) was capable of taking care of them. Shakti came forward and gathered the six bodies into one and lifted the baby with six heads.

Science today talks of gases swirling and combusting with extreme heat, and then cooling to form planets. The six heads are representative of the six directions or realms of the universe, the six time periods or phases of creation (the time it took for the universe to form from that nano second after Onkaar). In the Genesis, it talks about God creating the universe in 6 days.

This infant is called Kartikeya because he was tended by the six Kirtikas (the Pleiades cluster); Sharavanan because he was tossed on the shara grass; and Skanda because with him started space and time. Skanda also means that which has burst out or has been emitted, which has been poured out and effused. He is also consciousness, perception, and a concept. In South India, he is also called Kanda signifying that He bears the weight of the universe on His shoulders.

Mythology also says that He is seated on a peacock, whose colorful plume encompasses the shades of the universe and its span represents the open spaces which can absorb the positive and negative aspects of the universe. Spectroscopes, discovered in 1850s, have fanned out the peacock tail of starlight, which are being used by astronomers in every major observatory on earth today.

Now, it is said in myths that Lord Kartikeya delineated the meaning of OM to his father, the Creator. If that is so, why can't we know what OM is in Absolute Terms?

Yet another story from the same myth gives the answer.

OM – God becomes a Student

In the magnificent snow-clad mount Kailash, on top of the world, Lord Shiva and Goddess Parvati were resting. Their young son Kartikeya, not more than perhaps eight or nine, was guarding the door, so that, no one would disturb their rest.

Lord Brahma came seeking an audience with Lord Shiva. The Lord's son barred the entrance and would not let Lord Brahma pass. Lord Brahma got very upset and demanded to be let in.

"I will let you in provided you tell me the meaning of the Pranava shabda OM," said young Kartikeya.

Lord Brahma was getting angry by now, for it was the height of insult to be questioned by a lad when he was the one in charge of creation.

"If you do not answer, I will have to assume that you do not know its meaning," gently said Kartikeya.

Lord Brahma was in a quandary, for although he was entrusted with the task of creation, he really couldn't tell the exact meaning of all that it entailed, and the ramifications of OM. To hide his ignorance, he started arguing vociferously with Kartikeya. Hearing all this commotion, Lord Shiva and Goddess Parvati came out. Immediately, Lord Brahma launched into a complaint about Kartikeya's behaviour.

Lord Shiva turned to Kartikeya and asked, "Why did you stop him?"

"Because I did not want him to disturb your rest."

"So you asked him the meaning of the Pranava shabda OM?" Lord Shiva asked in disbelief.

Kartikeya nodded. "It would have taken him forever, and you would not have been disturbed."

"He was being precocious," interjected Lord Brahma.

"Do you know the meaning of OM?" asked Lord Shiva of his son, "for if you don't, it was presumptuous on your part to demand its explanation."

"I do know it," Kartikeya said quietly.

"Very well, then, tell me," Lord Shiva said, smiling in an aside to Parvati.

Lord Kartikeya became very serious. "If you want to know, then you must become my pupil. This is so deep that I can only impart it in secret."

Lord Shiva looked incredulous for a moment, and then he laughed. "Very well," he said, humoring his son, "I will be your pupil."

"This is serious," rebuked Kartikeya.

Lord Shiva became solemn at once and allowed Kartikeya to lead him into seclusion on top of a hill in the south. There, the Lord became a student and the son became a teacher to whisper the secret of OM in his ears.

Even today, a temple stands on top of this hill called 'Swamimalai' (hill of the Lord), where a role reversal took place.

Why did Lord Shiva pretend not to know when he himself was responsible for OM? It is said that he wanted to test his son's knowledge.

How come Kartikeya knew the meaning and not Lord Brahma? Because Kartikeya is OM. Lord Shiva emitted a spark off his third eye to create, and this spark became Kartikeya. This spark, this bindu (dot), this golden embryo (Hiranya-garbha), was Onkaara, which can be equated to the Big Bang. In scientific parlance, it has come to be called Lemaitre's egg, named after a Belgian cleric (also a physicist at Louvain University) who postulated it in 1920. He said that all the matter in the cosmos was packed into a single atom. He described it thus: "The atom world broke up into fragments, each fragment into still smaller fragments."

In the Bhagwad Gita, the Lord says:

"O Arjuna, I support this entire universe with a single ray of My boundless Glory." All scriptures talk of the Creator creating, using only a very minute portion of His power. If an infinitesimal power source is the universe, then it follows that it will be next to impossible to know that Absolute Power completely. It can only be known in bits and pieces.

Lord Kartikeya represents the six dimensions of the universe, i.e., inner space, outer space, limited space, unlimited space, visible space and invisible space. He represents the five senses and the sixth intuitive sense needed to understand the universe. All aspects of the universe that can be known in bits and pieces come under one or the other of these categories. The elements and time come under outer space, limited space and visible space. The enlightenment, revelation, timelessness and singularity come under inner space, unlimited space and invisible space.

All of them are immersed in OM. Each of the following chapters is devoted to understanding them.

Om is Sound

PRANAVA SHABDA

The very first expression of the Absolute Truth evolved as OM. It was the silent assent as in 'Mmm' or 'Hmm.' Therefore it is called the Pranava Shabda (the original sound).

Pranava - meaning, the original, the mysterious, the mystifying, the Life Principle Sound, the Word. This Life Principle Sound of the universe existed even before the universe itself, till God thought of the universe. It existed in its latent, soundless form, till it proceeded from deep silence of the formless as a Shabd, a Word.

All religions and scientists agree that the first moments of creation were in the realms of sound. The Vedas, Upanishads and Markandeya Purana state that the 'Akshara Brahma' or 'Shabda Brahma' existed free of space and time, with a limitless expanse of ideas within itself.

"In the beginning was Word, and word was with God, and Word was God," says the Bible.

In Sikh scriptures, It is called 'Naam' (or Name). God has been called the ultimate Naam, or OM because it is closest to the cause-less Brahm. In the Quran, 99 names of Allah are all important. Shabd, Word, Name is everything. It identifies everything.

The sound current or life-principle that flowed from that mysterious source is Om. The cosmos is created at Om, i.e. the starting point is Om. Indeed Om is with Brahman. OM is Brahman. Brahman is OM. Brahman is impossible to know. OM however, is possible to know. How? It occupies and girdles the entire universe in all its forms, says the Atharva Veda. We have access to OM through the elements, through the cosmos.

Because of the mysterious nature of Brahman, and Om's association with Brahman, it becomes mystical in origin.

From the cause-less Brahman, proceeds the causal universe and as such, both are one and the same. The sound current Om is the link between the two.

Om is the very nature of God, which caused this universe, not out of a personal will, nor personal desire, not even in play. It is caused because it is the very nature of God, and therefore, it just is.

VIBRATION AND RESONANCE

Once the Pranava Shabda was set in motion, it started vibrating outward. It started expanding and pulsing through every atom. Within every atOm is the hum of Om, and conversely, every little atom that has come into existence has done so with the vibration of Om. It is interaction between matter and energy (constant collusion of micro atoms) that causes it to vibrate. And it is this vibration or sound that pulses through the timeless universe. There is a continuous hum in the universe, and it is the same from every corner of the universe. The hum is literally hmmmm! This vibration permeates and radiates through the universe to this day. The vibration of Om is the source of all sound. This vibration is nothing but the universe becoming conscious of itself.

The voice of the physical body is vibration. The creative sound movement causes various levels of consciousness in a being. The being resounds in non-being and non-being vibrates in the being. What this means is, in a being is the universe of sound and in the universe of sound is the vibration of the being. We vibrate from the top of our head to the tip of our toes. The sound of our heartbeat is produced due to vibration. This vibration can affect the energy level in the body with the slightest change. The very breath we inhale and exhale vibrates with molecules around us and within us, causing a fluctuation in the atmosphere around us.

The hum of Om that vibrates through the universe also resonates back. Every sound reverberates through the universe and comes back as Om. Even if one cannot understand the extent, it can be felt. When Buddhist monks chant Om at a certain pitch, the air around vibrates and reverberates. When the Vedic hymns are chanted by priests in unison, when Catholic monks recite the Gregorian chants, the sounds vibrating are overwhelming and take you to quite another realm. The pitch, low or high, determines the cycles of vibration.

Sound is produced by hitting, pulling, stretching, scratching, rubbing etc. Musical instruments yield their notes through the displacement of air when a string is struck and the air travels as a wave. Whether it is a tinkling sound, air rushing, strings twanging, a high note struck, a wailing echo, all start with a hum and end as a hum. This vibrating hum in everything is Om.

Try a simple experiment by tying a string on a hanger and hit the hanger. You can hear a bell like hum. Without an amplifier, you would need to hold the string close to the ear. If you have an amplifier, place the string on it. The vibrating Om becomes very clear. This can also be experienced when a tuning fork is hit against a table. The hitting causes the table to vibrate. This can be heard better by immediately placing the fork on the table after hitting it and pressing your ear to the table. The sound waves echo through the fork louder. The hum of the sound waves is OM.

FREQUENCY

OM is the natural frequency of the vibrating universe. It is the pulsing energy of the universe as it is set in motion as sound or electromagnetic waves. Sound begins with vibration and travels through air as waves. Sound vibration can be divided into billions of waves. These waves travel as electric currents. Each wave has a shape, and a different field of energy maintains each. The difference in energy dictates different activity. Different activity causes different reactions. Waves are expressed as sin in trigonometry. Mathematics is the language used to express the coordinates of these waves.

Today we experience the way sound travels through waves when we talk on the telephone. A voice at one end of the world travels in waves and is re-assembled at the other end, causing different frequencies. The upper limit of normal human hearing is 20 kHz (kilohertz). Ultrasonic range is 20 kHz to 1000MHz (megahertz). A low frequency wave causes low hertz and a high frequency wave causes a high hertz (hertz is the unit of frequency, one hertz representing one cycle per second).

Frequencies come across as a sound wave because of the compression and expansion of air, or through the solids and liquids in which they travel. The frequency of vibration is in proportion to the energy an object puts out. A rubber band held in the mouth and pulled taut or loose at the other end changes the frequency of the sound. The higher the frequency, the shorter the waves. The electrical sound waves when scrunched together go up and down in compression waves.

Vedic scriptures declare the universe to be made up of spheres of nine triangle (Sri Chakra Yantra). Architects from ancient times till now, consider the triangle to be the most stable structural form. The pyramids, the temples of South India, the Mayan temples are all examples of this. In fact, R.Buckminster Fuller a prominent structural engineer, designed geodesic domes using triangles because everything is contained within triangles. The geodesic dome is made up of nine triangular segments, each triangle at 40° angles, making a 360° sweep. Modern architect, I.M. Pei used the triangle as the basic element when he designed the National Gallery of Art in Washington D.C. The waves on a heart monitor go up and down looking like triangles. Triangles are part of sound waves.

Every sound is a note. Each note is a particular frequency. Bats have ultra sound, i.e. they can hear sounds of very high frequencies. Humans cannot hear at such high frequencies because it will shatter their eardrums. High frequency notes literally can shatter glass. High frequency sounds occur when air currents are increased. You can experiment this with a fan's speed. A room with an echo also has high frequency. At very high frequencies, however, the echoes become distorted.

The hum of Om as frequency is there in all directions of the universe and it is constant and equal at all times. This hum could be a combination of all frequencies, although a single frequency could also be a hum. A single frequency can become monotonous, whereas a combination of many becomes harmonious.

Today, scientists like Arno Penzias have proved through radio telescopes that a background radiation hums through the universe from any given direction. They concur that it has been there from the start of the universe and is ever present.

When we hear the frequency of the universe through the medium of radio, television and the wireless, it is the original hum of Om. Unless tapped, the hum remains soundless. It also remains changeless and is the substratum on which sound is superimposed and travels.

PATTERN AND RHYTHM

The frequencies in Om are caused by cycles and in patterns. The vibration caused in any object reverberates in a set pattern depending on its pitch.

There is a mathematical precision with which the universe functions. The sphere of nine triangles making up the constituents of the universe represents three actors: space, time and causation; three ingredients (qualities): sattwa (stillness, truth, goodness, purity), rajas (passion, desire, activity), tamas (inertia, dullness, stupor); and three functions: creation, preservation and destruction.

This mathematical precision is part of our breathing, the beat of our heart and the beat of our pulse. We breathe 21,600 times a day. Our heart beats 72 times per minute. Our pulse beats an average of 72,000 times a day. 72,000 are also the small nerves that branch out from the main nerves of the heart. All these numbers are divisible by 9. This wonderful phenomenon is depicted in the architecture of the 'Chidambaram temple' in South India. This temple represents space, and every part of the temple describes the cosmic dance of Lord Shiva. There are nine golden kalasas (a ball with curved top). There are 21,600 golden leaves (tiles) and 72,000 nails holding these leaves.

Every formation of the universe is in precise patterns. The interaction of the matter at a cosmic level conforms to set physical laws. There is a recurring pattern to be observed in chemicals and physical reaction at a cosmic level. The same is also true of elementary particles. Om is the elementary sound of the universe. Every sound has a physical pattern. Therefore, you can say that Om is the design of the universe. It is what charts the course and the map of the universe.

Patterns in sound by their very nature are harmonious. The

repetitive patterns governing sound waves elevate one to a higher state of being.

A rubber band or string pressed on a table and held taut at the other end, when plucked will give an idea of repetitive, cyclical patterns. The patterns move in concentric cycles. This can be observed when a pebble is thrown in a pond. The ripples move in concentric cycles and the sound is very harmonious.

It is this sense of pattern underlying everything in the universe that creates rhythm. When Lord Shiva did his cosmic dance of creation, it was in rhythmical patterns. This rhythm is intrinsic to the beat the universe runs on. At the core is the single beat. The heart beats this single beat continuously, as does the clock ticking its seconds. But the heart beat also runs in cycles of four. Four becomes eight and eight, sixteen. In between you also have the odd beats, which are in threes. Once again, the human heart beats in three-quarter times, i.e. the gap between one heart beat and the next is a three-quarter measurement. Three becomes six, and so on. In Vedic language, it is called shadanga (meaning six parts) and shodasanga (sixteen parts). The Prasna Upanishad declares that the Self, after creating ether, air, fire, water, earth etc., created sixteen elements or parts, and then directs:

"The sixteen parts are spokes projecting from the Self, who is the hub of the wheel. The Self is the goal of knowledge. Know him and go beyond death." (IV – 6)

Everything disappears into the Self - the One. The odd numbers also run in patterns of five, seven and nine. Thus all the primary numbers are covered.

Pattern and rhythm are a direct result of sound. Mathematics is the language of the universe and when it converses, it comes out in harmonics.

NAAD – MUSIC

OM is music. The ancient Vedic scriptures declare that the universe was formed out of Naad. Naad literally means sound. But Naada also means melody, sweetness, and harmony. The universe was, therefore created in harmony, for harmony. The universe speaks to us in the voice of harmonic resonance. This harmony is the music of the universe. It is the music of the spheres. Wherever there are human beings, there is music. Animals are not blessed with this trait. It is human beings who generate music and find ways and means to use objects in the world to create music. Not only this, they use music to create harmony. Even when sound comes across as noise initially, when it gets subdued, you can hear the underlying harmony. A steel plate falling down, a coin rolling on a table- top or the floor, grates initially. But as the spinning starts to subside, the last notes fade away in harmony.

This harmony in music does have a soothing effect. When the mind is stilled with music (i.e., the breath is soothed and steadied with music which in turn keeps the mind at rest), the music of the universe vibrates in the lotus of the heart. Music soothing the beast is not just fiction. Every atom in the universe vibrates with the primordial sound. When the beast hears soothing music, it is in its nature to become one with the primordial sound and exhibit a state of harmony. This causes it to be in harmony with its surroundings and become calm.

The harmony accompanying Naad is called Sruthi (scale). The Vedas are called Sruthis – meaning, that which is heard. It is Sruthi that creates music and creates harmony. Without Sruthi, you cannot be in tune, and without tune, there is no harmony.

Sruthi is made up of seven swaras (notes). These are Sa Re Ga Ma Pa Da Ni. In Western music, they are called Do Re Me Fa So La Ti. Wherever music emerged, it was always on the basis of these seven notes. Each note has a place of its own and a meaning of its own. Of these, Sa Re and Ni, are the most important. Sa is the start of creation, called 'Srishti.' Ri is 'Rita,' the force behind creation. Ni is 'Nikashaha,' the light making creation appear. In the chants of the Rig, Yajur and Atharva Veda, it is these three notes, in the Raga Karaharapriya, that are strung together in patterns and repeated to cause harmony in body, mind and spirit. The Sama Veda uses all seven notes. Sama Veda, the Veda of music is responsible for the style and texture of Indian classical music, especially, Carnatic music.

The Gregorian chants use these very notes in an undulating style to create harmony.

The same can be heard when verses from the Quran are recited.

The four other notes Ga Ma Pa and Da, denote the following:

Ga – is the illusion of knowledge (gyan)

Ma – is the center of consciousness (manas)

Pa – is the hidden qualities of the universe, mind and wisdom (Purva, Paroksha)

Da – is the matter of which the universe is composed, (Dharti - that which is the Foundation, Stability, Link)

When Sruthi is set in the Sruthi box, Tanpura or any instrument, it is always set to Sa and Pa.. In musical parlance, Sa is called Shadjam and is representative of Shakti. Pa is called Panchamam and is representative of Shiva with his five faces facing five directions of the universe. It is also thought of as creative energy, melody and rhythm. Sruthi (melody) is mother, and layam (rhythm) is father. When the Tanpura is set to these two notes and is continuously plucked, the soothing hum of Om can be heard.

It is manifest that OM or Brahman hums through every note in the universe. The human body is but a vehicle for that musical scale to spring forth and blend into the spheres. The musical scale that hums within springs without. It is said in the Vedas that wherever there is divine music creating harmony, God or OM vibrates there. Harmony is associated with 'Sur,' meaning, to be in tune, and disharmony with 'Asur.' Sur also means Angelic and Asur means demoniac. Therefore, that which is in harmony, in tune, is Angelic, and that which is in disharmony, out of tune, is demoniac.

Sri Chandrasekharendra Saraswati (Shankaracharya) has extolled the virtues of Sama Gana (singing of hymns) as prescribed in the Sama Veda. "Recital of Vedic mantras not only produce beneficial vibrations in the pulse of the one who chants them...but also in the one who hears them." He further declared that the mantras are "set to music, which is greatly conducive to the spiritual evolution of the self and the grace of God."

Lord Krishna declared in the Bhagwad Gita:

"Vedanam Samavedosmi," meaning, Among Vedas, I am Sama Veda. (10-22)

Pythagoras summed this up beautifully when he said: "God is supreme music, the nature of which is harmony."

AHAT AND ANAHAT NAAD

Naad – the harmonious sound has two sides to it: Ahat and Anahat, i.e., there is manifested sound and unmanifested sound. The two are experienced on different planes. Ahat is sound which is physically heard, and Anahat is the unheard sound which is in the psyche. These two internal and external sounds are both creative and destructive. They can be one or the other, or both together.

Ahat, the manifested sound is that which we hear twenty four hours a day, our ears are tuned to receive sounds from various directions. Anahat, the unmanifested sound radiates, vibrates and hums within us. Ahat is called 'Shabda Brahm' and Anahat is called 'Ashabda Brahm,' i.e., the Word is God, and Word - lessness is also God. In other words, sound is God and silence too, is God.

For Ahat, there has to be an object hitting together, such as clapping of hands, hitting the cymbals together etc. Ahat is, therefore, the struck sound. Every sound we hear in our world is Ahat. It is the sound that emanates when the Life Principle OM in the body starts to make a sound. The fire (energy) in the body joins the air in the lungs at the bottom of the stomach called 'Nabhi' (near the navel) and passes upwards through the chest cavity and pushes the sound out through the mouth. Therefore, Ahat is sound produced through motion.

The essence of sound, however, is there in motion and silence. In motion, it is heard, and in silence, it is felt. Anahat, the silent sound is in the nature of the cosmos. It is felt as an after effect, like the air brushing through the bamboo shoots, the vibrations felt long after a gong has been sounded, when the mystical sound Om is chanted repeatedly and a vibration is felt on the lips.

When the first test explosion of the atomic bomb took place, Otto Frisch described the sound effect thus: "...It was an awesome spectacle; anybody who has ever seen an atomic explosion will never forget it. And all in complete silence; the bang comes minutes later, quite loud though I had plugged my ears, and followed by a long rumble like heavy traffic very far away. I can still hear it."

Whereas Ahat is heard only in a moment, the Anahat is ever present in the universe. That's why it is known as the Eternal Sound. Why Eternal? Because it existed in its latent form even before creation. And since we cannot comprehend the point before creation, for it is mysterious, we cannot define it. We can only describe it by negative qualifications like Anamika (nameless), Alakh (un-understandable), Akathaniya (indescribable), Agam (inconceivable), and Anahat (soundless); Anahat, because It does not make a physical sound and give us a clue to its nature. When we hear a physical sound, we can immediately identify it and say whether it is a flute, a car horn, a drum beat, and so on and so forth. But Anahat not only does not give us a clue to its nature, it is unidentifiable as one or the other sound. For e.g., when we strike a note on the piano, or play a note on the trumpet or violin, the fading sound is identical in all of them. It is just a hum. It is the union of sound and emptiness. It is, therefore, every sound in the universe. It is that stupendous hum of OM that runs through everything in the universe and beyond.

The faculty of hearing is continuous whether there is sound or not. It is attuned to hearing Ahat. But when one is able to ignore the worldly sounds and hear the intrinsic OM within, that is Anahat.

NADIS

OM is *Nadis,* which are the tubes or pulse points in the body. The Anahat flows through the ten *Nadis* in the physical form continuously. There are three major *Nadis* running through the spine and head through which Om as Anahat can be experienced. They are Ida, Pingla and Sushumna. They are connected with an unseen string and as the air of life pulses through them, the harmony of OM vibrates with the rhythm of life using varying frequencies, in sound and silence through our pulse eternally. It is there at a subconscious level all the time. To bring it to a conscious level, the three main Nadis have to be aligned perfectly to allow air to flow freely, without any obstruction. The Lord says in the Bhagwad Gita:

Samam kaayashirorgreevam dharayan achalam sthiraha
Samprekshya naasikagram swam dishashcha anavalokayan

"Holding the body steady, keeping the middle part of the body, neck and head in a straight line, a yogi should focus his gaze at the tip of nose, without allowing his gaze to wander." (6 – 13)

This way, when the oxygen reaches the brain, it benefits the body and psyche completely, enabling it to release the appropriate chemicals needed to create a sense of well being. This is at a physical level. At a cosmic level, these three important pulse points give a clue to the eternal nature of the Anahat. When the mind is trained to hear the Anahat, it is by using these three points. It is said that as Om travels from Ida, Pingla and reaches Sushumna, which is the seat of consciousness, one can have a brief glimpse into the eternal universe of Brahman.

The Nadis keep the rhythm of life. The lub-dub of the heart is heard through the pulse points. It gives an indication to the health and vitality of a being. The flow of Om through the Nadis is our connection to the invisible universe.

ARTICULATION AND KNOWLEDGE

Ahat and Anahat became entrenched in the consciousness of the being. While the whole universe hummed with Om, which is primarily an auditory symbol, it was left to human beings for whom it was a special gift, to develop that into articulation.

Articulation starts simply with Om or 'hmm.' If you listen carefully, it has all the vowel sounds - a e i u o. At the end of every such articulation, when the mouth is closed and the lips meet, there is an automatic 'm' sound. So, the vowels become Aaeiuom (AUM). Simply put, when the mouth is opened, 'Ahh' emerges, then the sound of 'Oo' fills it, and then, when it is closed, 'Mm' finishes the sound. This is very prominent when we try to fill in the gap between sentences. 'Um, um,' is the sound we make as we get our thoughts together. When consciously noted, the opening of the mouth commences from the larynx, the sound then passes through the throat and by the time the lips close, all parts of the mouth have been used. Every sound human beings and other creatures make, starts this way. In humans and cows, the Om is very clear, in others, it is there as vibration. Therefore, every sound in the universe is engulfed by OM.

Though it is commonly written as OM, the actual sounds heard are AUM. This is because OM has three parts and each letter in AUM implies one aspect of OM.

All sounds begin with 'A' or Akara. 'A' of necessity, is produced before other syllables.

'A' is the gross, physical body of the universe. It is an all-pervasive state and is bound to time.

'U' is Ukara, the middle state, which is the mental state. It is subtle and psychical and is the dream state. It is the state of expansive experience and is felt in space.

'M' is Makara, the third state, which is the causal state, i.e. of original 'Pralaya' or destruction. It has potential and is the measure of all things and the Self within. It is a dreamless state in which awareness of one's own state of consciousness evolves. AUM or OM, the comprehensive whole is a Transcendent or metaphysical state. It is the state where OM is indivisible as a syllable and the universe. It is One without a second and is the Supreme Good. It is the silence (Anahat) into which the universe disappears out of which it arose. It is a state where every atom in the universe becomes conscious of Pure Self.

AUM in modern times can be expressed as the Absolute Universal Mind (Manas or consciousness). Man is called Manushaha in Sanskrit. **It is made up of Manas plus anshaha. Manas, meaning mind, consciousness, intuitive awareness, and Anshaha, meaning parts, or Anu (atom).** So man is made up of atoms which become conscious of the physical universe and the universal mind. Simply put, Man (made up of atoms) is a being with consciousness (Manas).

AUM is also symbolic of the unknown and unknowable Creative Energy of the universe. Therefore, it is also expressed as UMA – Unknowable Mysterious Atomic (energy). UMA is known as the Goddess Shakti, which is the Creative Engergy or Pure Energy.

AUM is written in Sanskrit as ॐ The first curve) represents the gross state. The second curve) represents the subtle state. The handle ' represents the causal sutate. The lingering ँ (mm) sound represents The Absolute Truth. The many curves in the human body are molded in this shape: the eyebrows, the nostrils, the lips, the torso, the buttocks etc.

The Tamil AUM is written like the orifice of hearing Š.

The four parts of AUM not only develop articulation, they also impart knowledge and a sense of the universe. The first letter of Sanskrit is 'A' and the last letter 'H'. When the mouth is opened with 'A', 'H' escapes with the breath, and when it is shut, 'M' forms. 'Aham' in Sanskrit means 'I Am'. Between this first and last letter of the Sanskrit alphabet, all consonants and vowels reside, and in them, all knowledge which can be expressed through articulation. Knowledge developed in the universe as Apara Vidya (knowledge of this world) and Para Vidya (knowledge of the beyond)

Knowledge of the world found expression in words and knowledge of the universe in sound.

SPEECH - NAME

OM developed first as sound, then as articulation, and then as speech. With formation of letters, speech was not far behind. The physical being had developed mental capabilities. The heart is associated with peace and the brain with wrath, the heart with emotion, and the brain with intelligence. Interaction between the two caused speech to erupt. Once again, as with knowledge, speech developed as the known and the beyond. The two parts are called 'Varnatmak' (with words) and 'Dhunatmak' (with sound). The Varnatmak contained formation of languages, and therefore, differed in nature. That is, each language used its own undulations of sounds to create nuances. The Dhunatmak is beyond words, and therefore, the same everywhere. That is, the sound of thunder, the sound of air whipping through a forest is the same everywhere. Everyone hears the same sounds of the universe in OM, through OM.

Animals are restricted in their emotions and do not have the inner tongue necessary for speech. But human beings developed all the nine basic human emotions of courage, love, wonder, tranquillity (peace), laughter, fear, anger, disgust and compassion. All these emotions found expression in voice, words, talk, content, clarity of thought, and finally, speech. Both joyful and negative emotions of grief, wonder, disgust, fear, anger, joy are expressed by simply opening the mouth: Ah, Aha, Hmm, Hun, Ha, Oh, etc. All these again proclaim the beginning of sound. Hmm is the first sound for man or beast. This is because sound is produced only on exhalation, not inhalation of air.

Once emotions had caused speech to erupt, it identified objects and things in the universe. It came up with Nama or name. What's in a name? Everything. Everything observed in the universe takes shape in the human mind and is assigned a name. The French way of pronouncing name is 'Nom.' Om is inherent in it.

The assigned name is OM. Name – a label given to an object or a person. Every time a name is bestowed on anything, the hum of Om is set in motion. Name is a mark of identification. It differentiates one from another in the visible and invisible universe.

The need for name arose out of a need for discipline. First the creatures of the world got names. Then the physical features of the world got names. Then the vast open spaces with the sun, moon, stars and planets got names. In fact, we are still finding new things out there in the infinite space and giving them names. We are still naming new elements. All these came out of the mind of man. He identified everything as far as the eye could see, as clearly as his mind could ascertain. This enabled him to neatly plan his life. Little societies formed and named every inch of their lands. This enabled them to go on the paths they had named with freedom. Like lived with like.

Imagine if roads were not built, streets were not named, then chaos would ensue in our world. No one would know where to go, how to go. However, this does not extend to the course of the planets, sun, moon and the stars. Irrespective of whether we name them or not, they go about in an extremely orderly fashion. Naming them is important only to us as a point of reference. So, names became very good marks of identification.

However, that is not the entire purpose of name. Name also helps identify qualities: good from bad, dark from light etc. If a bottle containing poison were not labeled, it could result in unfortunate death. Name tells apart that which is ennobling and that which is low, that which purifies and that which corrupts, and that which is healthy and that which is harmful. Not only does name tell the difference in and around us, it also tells us what direction to take in life. Without proper direction, we will all be lost children. The name 'Mother' tells the child which direction to take while seeking comfort. The name 'Father' directs the child to the source of strength. The name 'Teacher' propels a child towards the source of knowledge. This is a four- fold process. Name is connected with Rupa, Asti, Bhati and Priya, (i.e. form, existence, knowledge and pleasing or bliss). An object identified by name is associated with a particular form and thus comes into existence, knowledge of which is entrenched in the human mind, which contemplates it with pleasure or bliss. Name, therefore, sets off a significant process of internal vibration evoking different emotions.

Every name has a corresponding form. OM alone has no form for it covers everything for all matter and seemingly empty space and beyond is simply vibration. When we name a form, our field of perception is limited and so perishable, our connection to that name psychological. When God creates a form, it is universal. Brahman is universal and does not, indeed, cannot belong to any one individual or clan. The only imperishable word to describe it is OM. It is called Akshara Brahman. A – kshara: meaning one which cannot be reduced, destroyed or lose its fullness. It is limitless.

In a 'nama' is contained the secret of the universe. It is written in Sanskrit as 'Namaha.' It can be taken in two ways:

'Nam ahah' – my name is 'That.' 'That' is 'Tat' in Vedic scriptures and Sanskrit, and 'Tat' is the name given to The Absolute Truth, i.e., 'Tatwa' (essence).

'Na ma hah' – is the other way to look at it, meaning, 'I am not.' The Encyclopedia Britannica describes an atom as mostly empty space. There is more nothing in the universe than something; even in what appears to be something, it is mostly nothing. The perception that something is solid and stationary is an illusion, for the electrons are moving so fast, they give the illusion of being solid. If the electrons stopped moving, then everything will vanish. In my pure essence, I am non-existent, only God is. I am not an entity; the only entity is OM or Brahman. This leads to the realization that without 'That name', I am a non-entity, therefore, I bow to That (Namaha).

HEARING OM

God is the Shabd (Word), Ashabd (silence), the atmosphere, the elements, the substance and the essence of man's life as OM.

Though the faculty of hearing is ever attuned to the sounds of the universe, it misses OM in all the extraneous harsh sounds that drown out the harmony underlying every atom in the universe.

So, how can we experience only OM in our daily life? It is the hum that is forever in the baby's ears as it is cocooned within its mother's womb. It is the hum that can be heard while swimming with your ears submerged. Are these the only ways to hear it? What happens to this eternal sound once you become earth bound?

Sages affirm it is still there. It is in the three Nadis – Ida, Pingla and Sushumna that run through the spinal cord and connect to the crown of the head. Sitting straight with the torso and the neck aligned and reciting Om, we can hear it vibrating.

An experiment has been tried to create this vibration on the hills of Scotland. Various harps and odd shaped string instruments were set on a meadow, on top of a mountain, at odd intervals. As the wind whistled through the strings, the vibrations produced were similar to the sound waves on radio scopes – the sound of the universe. Of course, everyone cannot go up to the mountains, nor have a collection of instruments. So, a simpler way to experience it is on a Tanpura, set to the notes Sa Pa Sa. Though it is set to only two notes, all the seven notes can be heard.

The sound of Om can also be heard through the rumble of thunder and the roaring of the seas. These express the explosive nature of Om. Running water, the buzzing of bees, the twittering of sparrows, the tinkle of bells or chimes, blowing the conch shell or the flute, holding a sea shell to the ear, however, give a divine experience of Om.

The easiest way to experience Om anywhere, any time is to simply cover your ears with both palms. It also indicates that the flow of blood within the body through the heart sings Om.

By pressing the thumbs to the ears, all sound is shut and one can experience the silence of Om. Through this Ahat and Anahat Om comes space.

Om is Space

VISIBLE UNIVERSE – THE SKY – AKASHA

Akasha is rendered by the sound of Onkaar and starts expanding and filling up the universe. With what? With the visible matter that rests within the infinite invisible universe, which hints at the many dimensions of space. Space has only one quality - **sound.**

Akasha, means space, ether, the primal quality or element that is infinite. Was this Akasha there before the start of the universe or did it come into being with the start of the universe? Both Vedic and Biblical scriptures say that darkness was everywhere before God started the universe.

"Darkness was on the face of the deep and God's wind stirred on the face of the water," declares Hebrew text.

The Rig Veda makes a mysterious statement, "Darkness there was at first by darkness hidden." (x.129.3)

The Shiva Purana states that "everywhere there was nothing but darkness." The Markandeya Purana, the Brahmavaivarta Purana, all state that at first there was just darkness, in which Brahman sat. In some places, it has been referred to as a void, emptiness, nothingness. Also as a light so brilliant, with the brightness of millions of suns, that it was blinding in its intensity and gave the impression of darkness, and that, though it was dark, it was packed with energy.

The scriptures also go on to say that while God shed light upon the visible matter, he also created dark matter. Now, space is not just the visible matter, but ninety percent of the invisible matter also. It is some sort of an invisible, insensible medium that allows light to penetrate and makes it possible for us to perceive the visible space and the darkness. This medium has come to be known as ether.

To answer the question, "Was Akasha there before the start of the universe?", we can only say, Brahman, the causeless One, existed before the start of space and time.

The Big Bang theory concurs that space and time came into existence with the start of the universe. It is conceivable that the darkness that permeated God's world before the start of Onkaar is different from the dark matter we perceive in space. All that the scriptures say with certainty is OM existed before Onkar rent the universe, a light so brilliant that it blinds you and gives an impression of darkness.

Maimonides, Jewish philosopher, physician and astronomer, and Nahmanides, Jewish philosopher, reached similar conclusions and postulated that the pinpoint of energy that started the universe set time in motion and also the space into which this time flows. At that point, the universe was contained in an infinitesimal speck and expanded into the infinite universe we see today. Then, it would have been impossible to perceive and comprehend that single point of energy even with a microscope. Today, the most powerful telescopes are insufficient to reach the infinite regions of the universe. To study the tiniest particles and microbes of the universe, even the microscope is not enough. Granted, we are still trying, and one day, may well succeed. But always, only up to a point, for we are limited by our finite vision.

This invisible universe or Akasha is still humming with Om or the Word of God from the time it was generated or shed light on. The hum is nothing other than pure energy. Therefore, space is subtle energy in which resides gross energy of matter, and matter is gross energy, in which resides subtle energy of energetic space.

OM is the limitless expanse of space in which everything exists as Om.

INVISIBLE DARK MATTER

We can see darkness vanishing into infinity when we look at the night skies. While the visible space is definitely humming with Om, it is the invisible dark matter that is reigning everything in and keeping it in its place. Ninety percent of the universe is made up of this invisible dark matter. According to scriptures, at the center of the universe is a void, a vacuum. Chandogya Upanishad says it thus: "Brahman is life, Brahman is joy, Brahman is the Void." (IV x 4-5) Science calls it a black hole. According to Einstein, at the center of a black hole is a singularity, and this singularity has zero volume. This black hole is so dense that light does not escape it. Yet, for all we are not able to see it, it is spinning the universe across a wide expanse in a cosmic dance of Om. It is the cosmic dance of Lord Shiva, which is pushing and pulling objects in space. It is the Chakra (discus) of Lord Vishnu, which is empty in the center, and yet, is spiraling outward, keeping the universe in its place. This spinning at extraordinary speeds is causing the universe to vibrate and resonate with the hum of Om.

Scientists today have concluded that the visible matter in space is not enough to exert enough influence to keep objects in their place. There is definitely more force in the dark matter than can be detected. Dr. Robert Kirshner, an astrophysicist, working on figuring out the mass of the universe has stated that "It will help in clearing the mystery of the dark matter and its gravitational effect on the things we cannot see." Dr. Lawrence Kraus, a physicist, elaborates, "Theorists believe 99% of the mass of the universe is invisible to telescopes. Now we learn that this dark matter, which may be made of stuff which may be different from anything we see on Earth, is the dominant stuff of creation. That means, if you took away you and me, and everything we see in the universe, the stars, and the real universe will still be there." What is this phenomenal power?

The answer lies in OM. It is Shakti (energy) of a kind unknown to man. Biblical scriptures call it the black fire.

The four forces exerting influence in the universe: the electromagnetic field, gravity, the higher and lower radiation, have all been ruled out as having enough power to hold the universe together. Though each in its place does influence the other, it is not sufficient to hold the entire universe where it is. There is, therefore, an invisible dark force that is exerting that influence. The Vedas call it OM. Imagine if you will, the universe as a discus and Lord Vishnu resting in the center, whirling it around with a very tiny amount of his pure energy expended. This is why, Lord Krishna (an incarnation of Lord Vishnu) stated in the Bhagwad Gita that he created the universe out of an infinitesimal part of his nature (energy).

Though it is not visible to human eye, it is said to be an energy field so powerful, it is blinding in its intensity, and yet, it doesn't burn one if one is fortunate enough to bask in its power. It is perhaps the light at the end of the tunnel, which gives a sense of well being. It is perhaps a force that can open up wormholes through which we can cross into different dimensions.

Rishis and sages were able to cross over to different Brahmands (galaxies, dimensions) in ancient times quite easily by using their powers accrued through meditation. The word they meditated on was OM. This OM is the invisible dark matter that girdles the universe and reels it in. Sages have declared OM to be the only medium through which the invisible dark matter can be breached. The Shvetashvatara Upanishad says:

"Meditate on Him as OM. Easily may thou cross the sea of darkness." (II –8)

In the Taittriya Upanishad, one sage who had meditated on OM, declared:

"I am Brahman, the self-luminous, the brightest treasure." (I –10)

Through Om it is possible to penetrate that invisible dark matter and reach that luminosity that lies hidden in it. It is the sounding of Om and hearing of Om that will lead one to and through the infinite space.

MICROCOSM/MACROCOSM (ATOM, ADAM, ADHAM)

OM is microcosm. It is the 'hmm' that vibrates and has set the universe in motion. God named the first human being Adam. In Sanskrit, he is Adham – the lesser being. Lesser than what? Lesser than God. With the Om humming and vibrating in him, he comes alive in the image of God, yet, he is not completely God. He can become God –like, but he cannot become God. So, he is Adham – the lower being. In Hebrew and Arabic, he is known as Adamah, and in Hindi, he is known as Admi – meaning man. Adam or Atom, as microcosm, they have the essence of Om humming in them. In the smallest of particles, Om hums away merrily. Om is there in 'Anu,' an infinitesimal atom, and yet the whole universe cannot hold it in, declare the scriptures. What does this mean? The Chandogya Upanishad elaborates:

"Smaller than a grain of rice, smaller than a grain of barley, smaller than a mustard seed, Smaller than a grain of millet, smaller even than the kernel of grain of millet is the Self.

This is the Self dwelling in my heart, greater than the earth, greater than the sky, Greater than all the worlds." (III – 14.3)

Adamah inhabits Vishwa (world, or mini-universe). This is microcosm. Vishwa is part of Brahmand (universe). That is macrocosm. If macrocosm were to fill macrocosm, then the whole universe won't be able to hold it. Therefore, the universe and everything in it always begins with microcosm. From a tiny dot seething with energy, the boundless space was formed and is still being formed.

The seeds of a tree may be very insignificant at the beginning, but carry within them all the elements of the tree. As a seed, it may bear little resemblance to the tree, but the ingredients are all there.

OM is quantum mechanics and infinite space. The physical and chemical reactions observed at the microcosmic level are happening at a macrocosmic level.

It is in man, in Adam made up of atoms that the two are reconciled. As microcosm, man carries within him all the elements of the universe, and thus becomes macrocosm itself. However, he functions in the macrocosm as the microcosm. Om, he is more. He is space and he is space-lessness too. At his core is simply OM, a void, no-thingness. This is why, the scriptures say that Brahman or OM is so powerful and big that the whole universe is not enough to contain It, and It is so small that the entire universe is contained in It. So, while OM is there in microcosm, in its expanded form (macrocosm) and beyond, the universe is incapable of holding it in and it can only abide in God. Thus, OM becomes Brahman itself.

PRESENCE (EXISTENCE)

OM or Brahman has come into existence. Om is felt as **shabd** or vibration in the union of matter and spirit. Every such union in the universe is vibrating with the same Om till it reaches back and comes to a full stop at the Uncaused One. So, when you say a thing has come into existence, it means, Om has started vibrating in that thing and God has made His presence felt. Here, the four questions asked by Aristotle are answered:

a) What is a thing made of? It is made up of atoms, which is OM.
b) What actually makes it? The vibrating OM or Brahman.
c) What gives it shape by which it is identified? The vibrating OM within the atoms gives it the shape.
d) What is the reason for it all?

This last one is not so easy to answer. It is tricky in that, it can never be ascertained fully by the limited human intelligence. Scriptures say the reason is also OM, which is the indicator of the Supreme Infinite Reality, which is divine and blissful. The blissful divinity can be felt however, through Om. Therefore, the presence of the universe signifies the Totality of existence in the form of OM.

Everything has come into existence for a purpose. The nuclear synthesis of the beginning took place at the exact time, the Earth was formed with exact requirements for life to exist, the creatures came into existence at the appropriate time, and the list goes on. That everything has come into presence by certain machinations of a Higher Cause is obvious. This is very easily ascertained by the simple exercise of going back from effect to cause. The Katha Upanishad says: "Go back from effect to cause until you are compelled to believe in Him." Everything stops at one point.

That everything works out to its full potential is also obvious. That is cause and effect. Everything has a prior cause and everything is effective. What makes it effective? Here it gets more complicated and the reason a thing is effective points to essence.

ESSENCE (CAUSE)

OM is the cause and OM is the essence. Essence is that certain something in everything that causes it to vibrate, live and have its being, by which it means: nature, shape, colour and smell. Is the essence there in a thing before it exists, or comes into being after existence? For example, the essence of fire is heat. Did the fire come into existence first, or did heat cause the fire?

This is the point St. Acquinas pondered upon and came to certain conclusions. He said that for a thing to exist, its essence must precede it. Let us call it Idea. Once the Idea has taken shape, it materializes into existence. Here Acquinas pointed out that it is not necessary for all Ideas to materialize. He gave the example of a Unicorn. The idea of a Unicorn is there, but its presence is yet to manifest itself.

So, the universe exists as essence, presence and the essence in every presence (power). Is God essence or presence or power then? If everything exists as an Idea first and then manifests itself, then of necessity, before God, there had to be some essence. But this would lead to a never-ending flight into the unknown. Therefore, God must, of necessity be the Ultimate Cause and exist as existence itself, with all essence complete in Him.

The Vedic scriptures say that above and beyond the essence is That which caused the essence to be present in a thing. It is different from the eight-fold composition of the universe: earth, water, fire, air, ether, wind, intellect (will) and ego. It is the source of all essence and existence.

The Lord says in the Bhagwad Gita:

Maya tatamidam sarvam jagat avyaktamurthina
Matsthani sarvabhutani, na chaham teshu avasthitaha

"The entire universe is pervaded by me in my unmanifest form
Although I am not within any creature
All creatures exist within Me." (9-4) And,

Parastasmat tu bhavonyaha avyaktaha avyaktat sanatanaha
Yaha sa sarveshu bhuteshu nashyatsu na vinashyati

"Greater than this unmanifest is another eternal unmanifest
which does not perish even when all elements (things and beings) perish." (8-20)

Here a distinction has been made between the one who caused a thing to come into existence and gave it essence and the Source or Cause. What this indicates is, though everything is part of that one cause, that One Cause is still distinct from everything, and therefore, is able to be the essence and existence in everything, and yet be beyond it all.

We can feel the essence, presence and power of the universe through Om. That is, since Om is the essence in everything, we can say, Om just is. But Om is also that by which this essence is manifested. So, every essence is the result of this Om. Om, therefore, is the source and Om is that which came into existence. There is no distinction between the two.

PERCEPTION (INFERENCE)

OM the visible space sets off our sensory perceptions. Knowledge of the visible universe begins with the senses, and through the senses, is imparted to the mind. However, perception is of two kinds: that which is directly perceived and that which is known through inference. That which is perceived depends on the world we live in: i.e., circumstances, our ideas, our beliefs and convictions. These shape our character and outward nature. There is scope for change as our circumstances, ideas, beliefs and convictions undergo change all the time. So, every time direct perception changes, the vibration in the body also changes. Our innate nature, however, does not undergo much change, for it directs our thought patterns as we perceive our world.

There are many things in life that are acknowledged through inference only. A simple example is, we cannot see wind. But when it stirs objects, we can infer that it is there. We know it through feeling. So, perception of the universe brings about a consciousness of the space all around us, which is permeated by a thin substance called 'ether'. This ether vibrates molecules and is heard as Om.

Skanda, the son of Lord Shiva, represents the five aggregates of the universe, which are:

1. Form (existence),
2. Feeling (consciousness – existence becomes aware of itself),
3. Activity (existence asserts itself),
4. Perception (existence responds and reacts to activity) and
5. Samskara, meaning cultivated, refined activity (perception gives rise to temporal reality where intellect, ego and mind are developed).

The developed intellect, ego and mind along with consciousness, perception and activity also represent the six faces of Skanda. Skanda is sitting on a Peacock. The spreading plumes of the Peacock are the open spaces and acceptance. The openness extends far and heightens perception through the beautiful colors of the plume. This is why Skanda, which also means a group or a cluster, is the symbol of OM itself. By associating space with Om, openness with Om, perception with Om, one is able to infer much that is imperceptible to the naked eye. This perception at visual level and through inference leads to knowledge of inner spaces.

INNER SPACE

OM is essence and presence. It is also the six dimensions of space – visible and invisible space, limited and unlimited space, and inner and outer space. Of these, the visible, the limited and the outer are easy to comprehend. What the eye sees, it transmits its vision to the brain. What the outer field of perceptions perceives, the mind cogitates on it. What the senses experience, they transmit to the brain in a limited way. The invisible, the unlimited and the inner space are the more difficult to comprehend. The invisible and the unlimited are tied to the inner space. If the inner space can be experienced, then knowledge of the invisible and the unlimited follows.

The essence that makes a thing what it is, is Om. It activates a thing from within. It is inner space. Man is able to experience this inner space up to a point. Whether beasts are able to do so, we do not know. It is only man who has this urge to conceptualize his visions of an eternal place of rest. Because of his extra sensory perception, only man is able to go into this inner space. How? He has the ability to relate his conscious perception to his own inner thoughts and feelings. He can link his experiences to perceptions out of this world. He can become conscious of the sublime nature of his inner being and connect with the cosmos.

Everyone has flashes of these insights. To become consciously aware of the inner spaces, one needs to become consciously aware of the Om vibrating within. To create this deliberate awareness, the starting point is to be aware of the outer hum of Om. It is to consciously enunciate and hear Om. Since the senses manifest outwardly, all our activity is directed outward. But the intuitive perceptive mind is also attuned to the voice within and seeks to break the outer barrier and go within. Once you have trained your outer self to hear Om continuously, the inner sound principle becomes easier to hear. When the connection is made with the inner voice, sound or Om, you become conscious of the Atma (soul), and the soul experiences itself. A being then is propelled towards outward thought, word and deed by the inner space at all times, consciously and unconsciously. Is there any proof of this? Yes. Messiahs like Jesus Christ, Bodhisatwas like Buddha, rasuls, prophets, sages, saints like Bernadette, Francis of Assisi, modern day great men like Gandhi, Shankaracharya, are all proofs of this phenomenon, where the eternal sound of the inner space of the universe directed their every thought, word and deed. For them, the outer had ceased to exist, only the inner mattered.

Modern day scientists like Dr. Philip Callahan proved that it is possible to go into inner space by repeating Om in a set pattern. There will be more about such experiments conducted in the chapter on energy.

CENTER

The most complex of concepts is "Where is the center of the universe?" If Om started at a point and started moving outward, then there has to be a core where it is strongest and holds everything in its place. The unlimited expanse that we see makes it hard for us to imagine a phenomenon so strong as to hold everything in its place from a central point. It has already been established that there is an invisible dark matter reeling everything in. Some called it gravity, but we know today that that alone is not enough to keep things in their place. Yet we know that there is such a force. A Hindu myth says Lord Vishnu is at the helm of the universe, holding it in its place with his Sudarshana Chakra. Chakra itself means circle. The Chakra can be a wheel with spokes extending everywhere, or a circle, which is Totality. The thing to determine here is whether there is a center to the universe, or is any place in the universe its center.

But then, God is everywhere. Om is everywhere, vibrating at the same frequency from all directions of the universe.

The truth is that OM occupies and girdles the entire universe, and so, we can hear it humming the same hum from any part of the universe, which the radio scopes of the SETHI project have proved today. Karl Jansky was the first to explore this at the Bell Telephone Laboratories in the 1920s. Today, astronomers have made a fundamental rule that our galaxy, the Milky Way is not unique or different from other galaxies. They call this the Cosmological principle, which assumes that the universe must be the same everywhere and in all directions. If this were not so, then there would be no uniformity of nature, i.e., the laws of physics applicable here on earth won't be applicable to the entire universe. The universe has no geometric center because it has no edges. However, for the universe to be held in place, there has to be an unmoved core. At its core, OM is said to be the Unmoved. That which has set everything in motion has to be immovable. So, the center of OM is inertial – where all values remain the same.

Then, where is this center? Let us start with our own planet. The Earth has a mysterious center, which is connected to the Milky Way. Our galaxy, the Milky Way, has a mysterious center, which connects it to the rest of the galaxies. Each cluster of galaxies has a mysterious center, and so on and so forth. Western scientists deemed the Earth's axis, which connects it to the pole star, as the center. The ancient Hindus thought of the center as the mystical mountain Meru or Sumeru, which stood directly under the pole star. For the Jews, it was the Holy rock of Jerusalem. For the ancient Egypt, it was the center cone of the Pyramids. This only shows that every human habitation thought of the Earth as the center of the universe. It is true and not true. While every mini-universe has a center of its own, any part of the universe is the center.

Astronomer J.J. Thomson came up with the raisin bread theory. When the bread rises and the raisins are spread evenly all over the bread, from any part of the bread, the raisin clusters on the bread look the same. In a similar manner, from whichever part of the universe we look at the rest of the universe, we will perceive the universe to be the same. So, we are not at the center of expansion, he concluded. Thus, from every vantage point of expansion, the law created by astronomer Edwin Hubble is obeyed, which is v = Hd, H being the Hubble constant, 'd' the distance between two points and 'v' the velocity of expansion.

A quotation attributed to Pascal, Bruno, Voltaire, Swami Vivekananda and many others is: "God is a circle whose circumference is nowhere and whose center is everywhere."

Perhaps this is why it is possible for Brahman to hold everything in its place because there seems to be no actual center. In the Brihadaranyaka Upanishad it is said: "Just like for water the one center (the uniting point) is the ocean, for touch the one center is the skin, for smell the one center is the nose, for taste the one center is the tongue, for form the one center is the eyes, for sound the one center is the ears, for thought the one center is the mind, for wisdom the one center is the heart, just so, for all beings, the one center is the Self." (II – 4 –2)

All the mini centers exert power to keep the universe going, and as the universe is expanding like a ripple in a pond, any portion can be the center.

"Anywhere is the center of the world," said Black Elk, a Native American chief.

While any place is the center, at the core is OM, the reigning power.

EXPANSION AND FULLNESS

OM is space. OM is expanding space. OM is fullness. The gap that we see in the vast open spaces is really not empty. There is energy of a different sort pulsating in there. That the universe is expanding has been established by astronomer Edwin Hubble based on the shift towards the red end of the spectrum of a receding star he observed in galaxies. He called it the 'Red Shift.'

As it expands, is emptiness left in its wake? No, say Vedic scriptures. As old Brahmands collapse, new ones take their place. The invisible dark matter fills up the empty spaces and sets Om humming again. Science says pretty much the same thing. As a star collapses, hydrogen rushes in to fill the void.

OM started complete, remains complete, and will remain complete. One of the core verses of the Upanishads is the opening invocation from the Ishvasya Upanishad:

"Om Purnam adaha, Purnam idam
Purnat, Purnam udachyate
Purnasya Purnam adaya
Purnam eva-vashishyate"

It means:

"That is full (complete, whole), this is full (complete, whole)
From fullness, fullness arises
Take fullness from fullness
Ever the fullness remains."

The key to the universe, God and OM lies in this verse. If we substitute 0 for fullness, the Matter becomes clear. 0 represents whole. That is 0 and this is 0. 0 arises out of 0. Take 0 from 0, and the remainder is still 0. An empty pot is filled with air immediately. The air that has filled the pot does not deplete the air in the atmosphere one iota. In a similar manner, what has been generated by God, still remains part of God, and therefore, is whole. And this generation in no way takes away anything from God, who remains whole ever. How can it when He states that the universe has been created using only an infinitesimal portion of His energy? OM or Brahman remains a constant, full.

Om is Air

PRANA – THE LIVING SELF

OM, God's winds stirred and sound vibrated through space. Wind makes it possible for sound to be heard. Wind or air controls and shapes our bodies. Wind creates frequencies. It makes it possible for things to live. It makes it possible for things to function. It makes it possible for us to feel. So, the two qualities of Air are **sound** and **touch.**

It is air that caused gases to separate and space to sort itself into its various components. This air was no ordinary breeze, but a wind that stirred up the universe. The sound generated was phenomenal. We can get an inkling of it by standing next to a powerful pedestal fan. The whirring sound heard is Om. We can stand in front of a less powerful fan and just utter 'Aaa.' The sound sorts itself out as a 'hmm'.

This wind intertwined and crept into everything as Prana or the living self. Prana is not just breath. Prana itself means vital force or Vayu. In the Prasna Upanishad, Sage Pipalada called it the primal energy, which is really the soul of the universe. It illuminates and animates everything. A Brahmachari (unmarried boy or man), who is inculcated in the traditions of the Vedas at the time of the sacred thread ceremony, is taught the importance of the five types of Pranas. The first is the main Prana, which dwells in the nose, mouth, ear and eye and is associated with the sun. The second prana is Apana, which rules the organs of excretion and generation, and is associated with the earth. The third prana is Samana, which resides in the navel and governs digestion and assimilation, and is associated with the ether. The fourth prana is Vyana, which moves through the lotus of the heart, the hundred and one nerves starting there, the hundred others from each of these, and the seventy two thousand smaller ones proceeding from these and is associated with the all-pervasive air. The fifth prana is Udana, which resting in the center of the spine is in charge of death, and is associated with fire. In what way is the Udana in charge of death? Life's breath goes out through the Udana at the time of death. It is directed through the heart, crown of the head or the lower portions of the body. Sastras say that depending on which portion of the body life's breath exits, the future life of the being is determined, and the being flounders or is uplifted accordingly.

Prana breathes and lives through life.

LIFE'S BREATH – VITAL FORCE (the animating principle)

OM is the vital force. Wind settles down as air once space has adjusted to perform its functions. This air starts off as pneuma or prana and then rests as vital energy within.

First God created Adam and then breathed breath into him, says Genesis 2-6. "Prana enters the body at birth," says Prasna Upanishad. Matter and spirit were harmonized by breath and caused an entity to live.

The Kathopanishad says:

"The being lives not by breath alone flowing in and out
But by Him in whom is the power of breath." (II – 2 – 5)

So, God not only breathes breath into Adam, He is breath itself. It is this Vital Force that enables one to breathe the air outside and live. As long as this vital force hums in a living self, it functions, i.e. it lives. This vital force determines the life span of all living cells. If you live, you breathe, if you breathe, you live. Once the Vital Force leaves the body, the body becomes inert, unable to inhale and exhale the air outside.

The main qualities of Prana are hunger and thirst. The living self hungers and thirsts for breath, food and energy. Every cell in our body is a living self. Every cell in the universe is a living self. Every living cell vibrates with OM, is OM. Every cell reaches for nourishment, which gives it the vital energy necessary to function. It is the energy absorbed through food. It is the latent energy within the body. The **psyche** and **psychological** and the **spirit** are activated through Prana.

The Celebes also believe in three aspects of the soul – the 'Inoso' or the Vital Principle; the 'Angga' or intellectual mind; and the 'Fanoana' or the divine element.

The body is a composite of the five elements and the correlating five senses. These, however, by themselves are useless. They need the animating principle to function. There is an amusing anecdote in the Prasna Upanishad, which tells about the boasting by the five elements in the body. Each claims that it is the most important element needed to function. The Vital Force scoffs at them and decides to leave. When it leaves, the others realize they have to leave, too. They realize their folly and accept defeat, knowing they are but a part of the Vital Force.

SPIRIT - PSYCHE - MIND

OM that vibrates through the being as Prana and absorbs breath as the Vital Force is divine in quality. For the ancient Egyptians, air had a spiritual quality. Certainly man breathed in air through his nostrils, which reached the lungs through the heart. But after this point, it was considered as the divine Vital Force that was distributed through the rest of the body, revitalizing the brain, and thus the mind. It is very easy to associate the Vital Force with the divine because it absorbs the colours of life. It is not dark in character. It has a spiritual quality because without that certain something the being loses its ability to live. That is, the ability to live is spirited away.

The air is our spiritual essence. It is the beginning of consciousness. The mind is very closely connected to the breath. When the mind becomes still, the breath becomes still. Here, by still, we don't mean ceased to exist, but, tranquil. Though it is a very difficult task to still the mind, yogis achieve it through meditation. They meditate on the very breath, Prana or Om they are trying to quieten. On a daily basis, individuals do manage to achieve this without any conscious effort on their part when their mind is absorbed in a task. The intense concentration in any given task momentarily suspends breath and stills the ever-agitated mind. In that moment and for a while thereafter, the breath takes the mind to a higher plane.

The converse is also true. If we regulate our breath and quieten our breathing, the mind becomes more centered and calm. An agitated mind causes an agitated breath, and a flustered breath stirs up the mind. So, the breath is the mind's connection to spirituality centered in Om.

SOHAM

OM is breath, OM is mind. What is breath saying to the mind at all times? It is saying 'Soham.' Soham can be split into 'So' and 'aham', meaning, **I am That**. Twenty four hours a day, with 21,600 breaths, the being reiterates Om. How? When we inhale, it sounds like 'So'. When we exhale and close our lips, the sound produced is 'hmm'. The inhalation is just a hiss, the actual sound produced is only upon exhalation. (All sound is produced only during exhalation.) Inhale 'So' – exhale 'hmm'. So – hmm, So - hmm, Soham.

'So' in Sanskrit means 'That', and 'That' refers to Brahman, God. 'Hmm' is representative of 'Aham', which means 'I am.' The inhalation is God and the exhalation is the being. Inhalation is going back to God, exhalation is coming out of God. The individual is affirming 'I am That' with every inhalation and exhalation. The suspended breath in between inhalation and exhalation is cessation, which is the Supreme Being. So, each breath becomes inspiration, cessation and expiration. We are born in every moment, live in divine presence every moment, and expire in every moment.

Soham, 'I am That' is signifying something with every inhalation and exhalation. It is saying that behind every breath, there is a Vital Force. In Sanskrit Soham is written without the 'a', which is implied. Delete the 'S' and 'H', which is 'Saha' in Sanskrit, and what remains is Om. 'Saha' means 'with'. The being, is therefore, with OM, which is the power behind the essence and presence. This is why scriptures keep reiterating that OM or Brahman is beyond essence and existence even.

Om, which is our breath, is the most natural sound in the world. It keeps nudging us towards who we are. That we are not far from the One That created us. Om is spirituality itself.

Om is Energy

FUSION

OM, Brahman has set the cosmos in motion. The Sanskrit word 'Srishti' describes this process as emitting forth. The emission of energy is let go, or sent forth to form and re-form. A resounding Onkaar shatters the quiet and fills out the darkness and is heard through the medium of wind. At the beginning of creation, before Onkaar rent the space, there was Pranava Shabda – the Supreme Brahman. It had within it both creative and destructive powers, called Srishti Pranava (creative energy) and Samhara Prananva (destructive energy). It also had another aspect to it – Ubhayatmaka Pranava (belonging to both). It was intense and it was smaller than 'Anu' (atom).

The Bible also talks of a darkness packed with energy, called 'Black Fire.' Physicists like George Gamow talked of a highly dense and hot small point at the crucial time between the start of the universe and nothingness. They called it the Big Bang. Cosmologists, Chushiro Hayashi and George Gamow developed the Big Bang model of the universe along with their colleagues in 1940-50s.

The Brahmavaivarta Purana talks of energy of millions of suns blinding everything and making it appear dark. Darkness and light were inseparable at that point. The Hymn of Creation in the Rig Veda describes it thus:

> "Of neither night nor day was any indication
> By its inherent force the One breathed windless."
>
> (x.129.2)

And then Onkaar exploded and Nada was heard and everything was encompassed within a field of energy (We hear the sound of thunder only after we see the flash of lightning, because the speed of sound is slower than that of light. Imagine the sound of the big bang. Before the enormity of such a sound – a phenomenal nuclear blast, the density of the pinpoint of energy would have been a very bright and powerful light). A seething cauldron of energy released its fierce force in all directions, fusing and moving apart and then coming together again. The Hymn describes a little later:

"Their rays stretched across...Creative force was there along with fertile power.

Below was energy, and above was impulse."

(Rig Veda: x.129.2)

What does this mean? It means, the rays of creation were stretched across the skies and the universe was forming above and below and in the middle simultaneously. The radioactive waves hummed and energy came together and separated in a game of hide and seek. Energy was within everything and impulse (matter) was coalescing. Space started expanding and allowed it to cool sufficiently to form stars and planets out of matter and gases. This fiery fusion of recycling goes on till today.

Of this process, the Lord says in the Bhagwad Gita:

Mayadhyakshena prakriti suyate sacharacharam
Hetunanena kaunteya jagadviparivartate.

"I sit on high, unattached and unbound by actions. I superimpose my power upon nature and she builds up and tears down – allowing the universal action to proceed and operate." (9 –10)

This energy which has the ability to convert into many forms is creative and fierce as fire (Agni), swift as electrons and protons, and destructive as nuclear atoms. It has three qualities – ***sound, touch*** and ***form***. The universe is adding new dimensions to itself due to this fusion of energy.

POTENTIAL

In that first moment of Onkaar, when the process of the cosmos expanding and cooling began, the potential for the formation of the universe in all its aspects was within it. From a thin insubstantial substance, the universe gathered mass and started forming tangible matter (much like the spider weaves its web out of a thin sticky substance).

"As the web issues out of the spider

And is withdrawn..." says the Mundaka Upanishad. (I – 1 – 7)

It kept withdrawing, changing and reforming continuously, and does so to this day. If matter is present, and changes to matter take place, it is a sign that energy is present. It is a change in the physical or chemical property in the matter. For example, if we leave ice in a heated room, it dissolves into water. If we heat the water, steam rises out of it. It is energy changing the shape of the matter.

The endless possibilities of change within matter, man observes within himself today. The growth of the human mind has been immense, and the possibilities seem endless.

Man may seem an insignificant part of the cosmos, but he has within himself the potential for all aspects of OM: Ananta (infinite, endless), Sat (truth, that which is), Chit (universal energy, consciousness), and Ananda (bliss). 'Anda' at the end of Ananda signifies an egg. Brahman created the universe out of Hiranyagarbha (golden embryo) or egg, and hence it is called Brahmanda. Brahmanda can be split into Brahma Ananda, meaning Brahma's Bliss. So, the universe created by Brahman is bliss. OM is bliss itself.

In a lesser capacity, man has the ability to mimic this creation by creating Pinanda (individual born out of an egg or embryo). This potential energy in man is endless.

"Tao begets one, one begets two;
Two begets three; three begets all things."

This Taoist philosophy is echoed in all world scriptures. This facilitated for endless creation.

ACTIVE PRINCIPLE (Mover and the moved)

OM that hums is the energy within everything. It is the Vital Force that allows us to breathe in the air. It is the Active Principle that charges and re-charges us and propels us towards activity. It is in truth that force within that performs the functions of our body, for it is what inspires our breathing, directs the digestive system, maps out the brain and introduces memory and knowledge in a being. It is also that which takes it all away.

Everything that is moved is done so by a power. For example, fire came into presence and its essence is heat.

However, if it is not moved (i.e., kindled), then it is simply there. That is, first there is name. But name alone doesn't do anything. Fire is the name. So, a quality is added to it – heat or energy. That still doesn't do much unless it is moved to operate. The power that moves it to work out its potential is OM.

Though the nature of Om (spirit) within everyone is the same, and everyone has the same potential source of immense energy, the energy level fluctuates according to thinking minds. Hence the variations in activity. The same is true of things, though not because of mind potential, but because of the nature of that thing. Hence the variation in formations of matter.

Newton's first law of motion states that an object remains at rest or in uniform motion, that also in a straight line, unless acted upon by another force. The other force of necessity must be unmoved, for if it were to move, then it cannot be the mover. The other object must be steady and strong to be able to move objects freely and at the same time, exert enough control.

OM as the mover is still and steady within matter, but as the moved is perpetually in motion. Therefore, it is said that the core of OM is inertial where all values remain the same. When one relates OM to Brahman, the matter becomes clearer. The Kathopanishad says:

"Though still, he moves everything everywhere." (II-21)

The Ishopanishad elucidates further:

"The Self seems to move, but is ever still.
Seeming far away, it is ever near." (5)

Brahman is the mover and the moved. How can It be both mover and the moved? Ishopanishad describes this power further:

"He is within all, and he transcends all." (5)

Brahman is above and beyond everything. It is without qualities. It is the Power that is at rest. If it were not immovable, then there would have to be another first mover that would move it. This correlates to God's essence and presence.

Physicists correlate it to a photon, which has a mass while in motion, but has no mass while at rest. It is both a particle because it has a mass while in motion and occupies space, and it is a wave because of the frequency of vibration that is in proportion to its energy. So, it is in a sense, both the mover and the moved.

Unlike the photon, however, Brahman is not caused and is purported to be beyond matter and energy. It is the Active Principle, the Unmoved and the Uncaused. The Shvetasvatara Upanishad reveals:

"There is nothing higher than Brahman...
He fills the cosmos, yet he transcends it." (III. 9-10)

PURE ENERGY

OM is pure energy. Energy takes form as fire, electric energy, magnetic energy, chemical energy, atomic energy, sound energy, light energy and radiant energy. Of all these forms, radiant energy is called pure energy because of the capacity to heat, burn, radiate, magnetize, vibrate and light. The Gayatri mantra talks of this Radiant Energy as being all in all: 'Bhargo Devasya,' it says, meaning, the Effulgence of the Creator. The sun, which has solar energy, has this capacity, and is equated with pure energy.

This is the divine breath the Egyptians talked of. The pure, undiluted, divine OM that vibrates within our being and radiates outward, warms us and keeps our bodies pulsing at a steady temperature and draws an invisible shield around us. It is the informing energy of all things. It directs and performs in the universe.

Dr. Fritz Albert Popp of the University of Marburg, Germany, discovered that all living cells emit a laser like energy that is cohesive. This energy is used by the system like a control center for all living processes. What is more interesting, he found out, is that the cells in the living body communicate with each other through the means of this laser light (i.e., they communicate with each other by releasing laser energy). This energy is released not only in visible band, but also in infrared band. This is interesting because the infrared band, which has 17 octaves of energy and is incoherent. For something coherent to be heard at an incoherent level is amazing.

What is more amazing is that even our electricity is measured in Ohms. Om seems to be in every cell of the universe. It is the home of OM and is at hOMe in OM. Once the cell is reduced to nothingness, and it is viewed with a microscope and enhanced and broken down, what ultimately remains is pure energy.

COMPLEMENTARY FORCES

Brahman created this universe and split into two – male and female, God and nature – the complementary forces of the universe. In feminine energy is the fertile ground that allows for creation to continue. This is why in every Purana, God is seen as splitting in two: as Radha and Krishna, Parvati and Shiva (Ardhanarishwarar). The Brihadaranyaka Upanishad describes this split thus:

"In the beginning this world was Self alone...He had no delight. Therefore one who is alone has no delight...He caused that Self to fall into two pieces. Therefrom arose husband and wife." (1.IV. 1-3)

The one became two, two became one, and the process continues. This fusing process generates energy, which hums with the vitality of Om. In duality is non-duality, and in non-duality is duality. They were not competing forces at the time of creation, but complementary forces come together for the purpose of creation. For creation to continue there had to be two of every kind.

In Buddhist context, they are regarded as wrathful energies in the sense that they represent hope. This hope is the cause of the perpetual creative forces of the universe. The wrathful energies here can be taken as passion or force, but because they represent hope, they are considered neutral energies. Neutral energies continue constantly and neither good nor bad accrue to them, or belong to them.

In view of this, though these energies are opposites, as creative forces, they are considered complementary forces or similar forces. Just like the energy that runs through all the bulbs regardless of their shape and size is one, the energy pulsating through these two forces is one. They are Yin and Yang – darkness and light, male and female, in harmony with each other and the universe. The act of creation itself complements the forces within it and Om pulses through at every point.

OPPOSING FORCES (Duality – Action and Reaction)

OM is buzzing with the hum of creation. While the complementary forces complete and carry on the task of creation, the opposing energies within them also cause dualities to envelop every walk of life. If there is a front, there is a back. If there is up, there is down. If there is a Creator, there is the created. These are at the opposite ends of the spectrum.

We know that atoms are made up of protons, electrons and neutrons. Each element has been numbered according to the number of protons in it. An atom in iron may have same number of protons, but the neutrons may differ causing more varieties. This also makes atoms with different atomic numbers behave differently. So, from complementary forces of nature, atoms become individualistic in nature, with traits of their own, each with its own functions. This leads to differences, and these differences cause opposing energy. Thus night and day, while being complementary forces, suddenly become two ends of the spectrum, unable to meet.

It is in the nature of male and female cells to walk the dualistic side of nature, even while colluding to keep creation alive. This difference causes a chain of reaction.

Because these opposing forces start competing for space, the needs of each give rise to different actions, and different actions give rise to different reactions. Sometimes, however, the opposing forces colliding can have a good result, like the triumph of good over evil.

Skanda's peacock destroys the serpent. This is representative of the fact that Skanda himself has broken the serpentine wheel of time. He is the eternal force that pierces through the veil of human experiences, which leads to the Ultimate Truth.

What this means is that there is a thin line or veil separating the pairs of opposites, or duality.

This veil can be penetrated with the power of Om. The opposing forces have to have a common ground of reconciliation, else the universe would not survive. Imagine if there had been only gravity, then everything would keep collapsing into each other, and nothing would get created. Imagine if the power that allows the universe to expand were so fierce that objects in the universe keep speeding away from one another with the same velocity they started at, without slowing down, then there would be no working universe today. It would be a vast, infinite, cold place. The fact is that there is give and take between the forces of gravity, electromagnetic waves and the nuclear radiation in the center, which keeps balance. Likewise, everything in the universe has two inevitable sides to it, and according to the requirements of creation, the two are always reconciled by the power of Om. Om it is that vibrates through darkness and light.

Lord Ganapathi stands for the reconciliation of opposites. His huge body and elephant head, represent the macrocosm, and his small legs, the microcosm. Yet, both are present in Om.

Thus, complementary forces work towards similar goals, and while opposing forces seemingly compete, they are there to reconcile the pairs of opposites and keep balance.

EVERYTHING AND NOTHING

If OM was a seething mass of energy, and Onkaar, the explosion of that energy, it stands to reason that it came from something. What is this something? The Lord says in the Bhagwad Gita that everything He has created has come forth from a fraction of His Power. Some translations substitute 'an atom' for a 'fraction'. It boggles the mind to think of a Supreme Being capable of bringing forth this enormous universe into existence with only one atom of His. However, if we think in terms of a pinpoint of energy, it is easier to comprehend. That one atom contained everything and nothing needed for the universe, just like the entire genetic code of a baby is contained in the sperm and egg. So, when we say OM is everything and nothing, we have to qualify the 'nothing' here as a 'void' or 'non-existent'.

The non-existent is Brahman. How so? Everything has come into existence because of Brahman's essence. So, the cause of everything is Brahman. Brahman is therefore, without a fore-runner, i.e., there is nothing before Brahman. Hence, Brahman is the Self-Existent One from whose essence, existence takes place. As the Self- Existent One, It becomes Pure Existence itself, because it alone is indestructible, while existence is temporal. And since It is formless, it is a void and called non-existent. It has to be a formless essence, for all forms proceed from It. If It had a form, then only the like could come out of like. A human can only produce another human, a bird only a bird, a fish only a fish, and so on.

It is important to note that it is the formless Brahman that vibrates as Om within, which directs life. If it had form, it would be very difficult for it to reside in a being. It had to reside as spirit. It is in the no-thingness that there is great value.

"Thirty spokes unite in one nave...wheel...
Therefore, on the one hand we have the
Benefit of existence, and on the other
We make use of the non-existence."

This Taoist verse discloses its deep-rooted philosophy that it is in a vessel's emptiness that you find its effectiveness. It is this void that enables us to hear Om, like a vacuum in a flask.

This is why Plato said: "Everything is becoming, nothing is." Everything is constantly dissolving and forming again, but the Self-Existent nothing, simply is.

Parmenides (Greek philosopher) thought that it was contradictory to say 'nothing' exists. How could 'nothing' exist? If it existed, then it was something. Therefore, everything had to come out of something, and everything must have always existed.

Everything did come out of something, and always existed as essence or idea in the non-existent One. Life, food, mind, knowledge and joy – these are all part of the existent and part of non-existent. They are everything and nothing. And they all vibrate with Om.

Om is Light

MANIFESTATION OF THE UNIVERSE

When Onkaar rent the cosmos and the universe started expanding through space, the universe became visible because of light. This manifested universe is OM.

"And God said let there be light," says the Bible.

"At first there was nothing. There was only a light with the brightness of millions of suns which gave the impression of darkness," says the Brahmavaivarta Purana.

When the first atomic bomb was tested in New Mexico, by J Robert Oppenheimer, many witnessed the event and described it in terms of a brilliant light at first. Otto Robert Frisch, a nuclear physicist, who was deeply involved in the experiment, felt as though the desert was shimmering in a very bright light. "The light did not seem to change for a couple of seconds and then began to dim. I turned round, but that object on the horizon, which looked like a small sun was still too bright to look at..." said he of the test explosion.

The very first atomic fusion, which caused the universe to explode into being, was a brilliant mass of light. It was a black fire that emitted no light. Through this darkness, which was OM, emerged the manifested Om. Its vibrations rent the universe and it was subsequently followed by a warm, glowing light, which is the sun, extending its rays for eons and eons.

Sahasra yugaparyantam ahaha yat Brahmanaha viduhu
Ratri yugasahasrantaam tehoratravido janaha

"Those who know that one day of Brahma extends for a thousand Yugas, and a night of Brahma extends for a thousand Yugas, are the knowers of day and night," says the Lord in the Bhagwad Gita. (8 – 17)

The Bible also says that with the Lord a day is as a thousand years, and a thousand years as a day.

Thereafter, the worlds made and re-made themselves, says the Brahmavaivarta Purana. It is described as Brahma inhaling and exhaling the Brahmands (mini universes). This process of creation and destruction of worlds, say the Vedas, goes on at the end of every Kalpa (one Kalpa is one day of Brahma). Currently we are in Shvetavaraha Kalpa.

"With the coming of the day, all the manifested beings and objects come from the unmanifested, and with the coming of the night, all the manifested go back into the unmanifested," it is said in the Bhagwad Gita. (8 – 18)

The day and night mentioned here are that of Brahma. So, God creates the universe in His one day and destroys it by His night. For us, it may seem like forever in earth years, days and nights.

The sun appeared only on the fourth day, corroborates the Bible. In the first three days, the

"Blessed One created and destroyed worlds."

Both in religious and scientific terms, everything has in it the stuff (matter) of the universe, and life is required to produce and re-produce itself. This manifestation of the universe becomes an ever-continuous process.

The question here is, did God shed light on what was already there, or did He shed light on everything after He had created it (i.e., after it had formed)?

The answer is - both. The universe is made up of the visible and the invisible. God split a very minute part of Himself and became God and Prakriti (nature). 'Pra' stands for that which is visible, and 'kriti' stands for that which is created. So, the visible creation became discernible only after God shed light on it. For God, the creation is always with Him, and, in that sense, it can be said that He merely shed light on what was already there.

Modern science confirms this. Once the Big Bang had set the universe in motion, and the thermal energy of the photons fell to 3000 K, the electrons were able to bind in stable orbit around hydrogen and helium. This enabled the photons to break free from matter and stand back as it were and shed light on matter. So, the light (photon) shed light on the manifested matter.

Om is the vibrancy of this light. We come from a plane where the light came into existence through itself to manifest creation.

SEPARATION

OM as the vibrant electrons had separated from its counterpart, the photons. The light in Om, i.e. its effulgence, illuminated and differentiated everything in the universe. While it was energy that propelled everything into motion, it was light that caused the distinction in different moving objects to be visible. It differentiated matter into its various components of essence, existence, sound, space, air, energy, water, earth, life, mind, senses, food, vigour, karma, austerity and revelation.

The sequence can be seen as follows:

Essence	shed light on	Existence.
Existence	shed light on	Sound.
Sound	shed light on	Space.
Space	shed light on	Air.
Air	shed light on	Energy.
Energy	shed light on	Water.
Water	shed light on	Earth.
Earth	shed light on	Life.
Life	shed light on	Mind.
Mind	shed light on	Senses.
Senses	shed light on	Food.
Food	shed light on	Vigour.
Vigour	shed light on	Karma.
Karma	shed light on	Austerity.
Austerity	shed light on	Revelation.
Revelation	shed light on	Knowledge.
Knowledge	shed light on	Wisdom.
Wisdom	shed light on	Essence.

Vigour translates into activity, and therefore, is the forerunner of Karma. Activity is the key to the running of the universe. Every action has a reaction, and thus, the universe seems to function endlessly. However, it is karma that sheds light on austerity, which paves the way back to essence. What starts with essence, ends with essence. OM is the essence, and it becomes existence and sheds light on wisdom through knowledge. (The gist of this sequence is in Taittariya Upanishad: II.1)

EFFULGENCE

OM is light. OM is radiance. OM is brilliance. Without light, the universe wouldn't be visible. Without light, the contrast between light and darkness wouldn't be obvious. Without light, for the creatures of this world, whose senses are tuned outward, the universe wouldn't make sense. Om separates light and darkness to maintain balance in the universe. Light is the sign of the awakening world, and darkness, the sign of the sleeping world. The awakening world is a world of activity and movement. The sleeping world is a world of rest and rejuvenation.

But OM is beyond this simple light. It is mysterious. It is powerful. It is mysterious on two counts. It travels as light from a source of phenomenal energy, and yet, when it illuminates, it does so with gentle warmth. Secondly, it has some kind of mass for it to travel distances, yet, when it touches the surface of any matter, it cannot be picked up or grasped. The simple example of light from a chandelier spilling on to a tabletop will reveal this fact. The light can be seen, but it cannot be gathered, nor is there any residue on the table to be wiped. Yet we say light is spilling on the tabletop.

It is possible for the light to be so because it comes from radiant energy. OM in its intensity is white in colour, for in it are contained all other colours. In fact, it absorbs all other colors. Thus, it becomes radiant effulgence.

The ancient Vedic Gayatri Mantra concentrates on the effulgence of the Creator in three parts. The mantra is short with a total of twenty- four syllables, but it covers all aspects of the creation comprehensively. It goes thus:

OM bhur bhuvah svaha, tat savitur Varenyam
Bhargo devasya dheemahi dhiyo yo na prachodayat

The first part contemplates the infinite glory of light that illuminates the three worlds – bhur (earth), bhuvah (skies) and svaha (skies); i.e., the lower, middle and upper segments of space.

The second part concentrates on the effulgence that flows from the Creator, because of which, the sun, moon, and the stars shine.

The third part humbly requests guidance from the effulgent spirit to guide and stimulate our intellect in the right direction.

The living cells in the body communicate through emission of laser light, which is effulgent. This emission is caused by vibration and vibration is Om.

It has been proven by Dr. Philip Callahan at the University of Florida, Gainesville, that repetition of Om and the Gayatri Mantra with a steady meter makes molecules release laser light, which is picked up by receptors in the body (acupuncture points in the body), and this in turn is fed back into the body. This alters the chemical make-up of the body, elevates consciousness and gives a sense of well being, a state of bliss.

INTELLIGENCE

OM vibrates in the physical body and the body of the universe. OM causes light to emit through this vibration. This vibration makes the universe and its beings conscious. Consciousness stimulates the intellect. The awakened intellect is nothing but light. Science has come to the conclusion that the secrets of the universe are largely in light.

Dr. Fritz Albert Popp explained that when the living cells emit laser light, they are picked up by receptors in each cell and are decoded and deciphered. This is the innate intelligence awakening. Every such emission and decoding process causes a light to go on in the cell, in the being. So, in a sense, intelligence permeates the universe as light.

This intelligence is manifested from the lowest to the highest organisms. When we are sick, the cells communicate with each other and before we know it, have sent hordes of combative cells to fight the disease. This happens 24 hours a day without our knowledge.

Through MRI scans, we can see electrical impulses dancing through the neurons imparting multiple ideas all at once from the different senses. Because the cells are sending myriad images flashing at any given point according to the desires initiated by the senses, intelligence in cells is manifested in different ways in every being. In some, there is excellence in science, in some, it is mathematics, and in yet others, it is music and arts.

There is even excellence in nature and natural formations, which take our breath away. Wherever we see such excellence – like the scent of a rose, splendour of the rising sun, the gurgle of an infant, all these signify the outstanding intelligence of Brahman. In the Bhagwad Gita, the Lord declares that the superlative in anything, be it a creature, mountain, river, flower, planet or galaxy, is so due to His splendor.

Yat yat vibhutim stavam shrimadurjitameva va
Tat tat eva avagacha, twam mama tejonshasambhavam

"Whatever being is endowed with glory and brilliance and vigour, know that I have manifested from a fragment of My Divine Glory." (10 – 41)

From the above it may seem that God's intelligence resides only in that which is excellent. However, while through excellence in anything we can perceive Brahman and hear Om vibrate at a very high frequency, for it stimulates our interest, there is intelligent light shining in every aspect of the universe, which enables us to perceive it. In every object in the universe, the effulgent radiance of the Creator shines through.

CHORDS OF CONSCIOUSNESS, KNOWLEDGE AND BLISS

OM vibrates through the three main Nadis (chords or pulse points) that run from the base of the spine to the crown of the head. The essence of this vibration is consciousness. It runs through the entire universe and connects the gross with the subtle plane. This conscious vibration allows proper air- flow to cool and warm the blood as necessary.

Om regulates our breathing every second, every minute of the day, and this regulation illuminates the chords of consciousness, knowledge and bliss in human beings. Human beings (to our knowledge) are the only ones to become conscious of themselves and the universe, to have some knowledge of the universe, and to experience bliss through this conscious knowledge.

The central chord in the body (called Sushumna or the central Brahma nadi) connects the nadis from the base of the spine to the crown of the head. It allows Prana (breath or Vital Force) to travel along with the Kundalini Shakti (energy, which is situated at the base of the spine) and the mind, to the crown. Therefore, Yogic postures insist on perfect alignment of the spine to allow air to flow freely through the body. This allows the mind to be tranquil and to experience Sat (Truth, Knowledge), Chit (Consciousness), and Anand (Bliss). This is attained through 'Tapa'. The original Sanskrit meaning for Tapa is heat. But Tapa is also associated with Tapas, which denotes ascetic practices and meditation. Meditation generates heat, and thereby, light or illumination. The Hopi Indians called this spark of consciousness 'Tawa' or Sun Spirit. They believed that the Great Spirit struck a spark of consciousness into space when creation took place.

The breath taken through the left nostril called 'Ida' or the 'Chandra' (moon) nadi, allows the body to cool. The breath taken through the right nostril called 'Pingla' or 'Surya' (sun) nadi, causes the warmth in the body.

The Sushumna nadi makes one conscious of the universe. The Ida, which cools the blood, is level, and therefore, responsible for creating knowledge. With every breath we draw, we increase our knowledge. The Pingla, which warms the blood, makes the being rest in bliss.

Through these nadis, Om surges as energy and illuminates in an ever-continuous pattern. Therefore, the learning process never stops till the end of life. The curiosity about the universe and life continues forever.

The nadis are directly connected to the mind. If the mind is unstable, the nadis do not perform well. That is, the churning mind does not allow the Vital Force to move freely through the nadis. Therefore, a positive mind is very essential for the nadis to open up. A negative mind clogs up the nadis and throws them out of sync, causing the being to become apathetic and no longer in a state of blissful consciousness.

THOUGHT

A thought is like a lightning. It is swifter than the wind and races forth on light impulses called OM. Light sheds light on the universe and the manifestation of existence. Light causes awareness to spring in every atom of the universe and causes consciousness to awaken. Consciousness gives rise to thought and intelligence.

When a being becomes consciously aware of the universe and garners knowledge at will, the mind races with thoughts every second, twenty four hours a day. The racing mind starts the being on a journey of experiences. No experience is possible without the cognitive ability of consciousness. Consciousness, in turn, makes the being aware of the universe, of the various nuances of the universe. This awareness causes confusion in the mind, for it senses life at a subtler plane, along with its gross existence. Out of this confused awareness, a need for the spiritual is generated. The agitated mind directs the thoughts towards the speculation of Brahman, Om and the universe. This spiritual need invokes the contemplation. Contemplation is possible only through Om, and understanding the Om, which vibrates within us.

Contemplation starts with a thought. Brahman is a thought. Om is a thought. The universe is a thought. It does not need avowal from human thought to be effective. It is effective on its own. But human thought needs Brahman or OM to be effective.

Thought power is very important. It can make us or mar us. It can lift us high or tumble us low into the depths of despair. It can enrich us, energize us, and sanctify us. The human mind is capable of noble and ignoble thoughts, which stem from the three gunas (qualities or traits): Satwa, Rajas and Tamas. Satwa is the pure state. Rajas is the passionate, desiring state. Tamas is the ignorant, dark state. At any given point in its life, a being is capable of maintaining any one state, or a mixture of two states. The more the positive thoughts are encouraged, the more the mind is uplifted and enlightened, and feels a lightness of being. There is a pun here on the words enlightened and lightness. Enlightened also means literally lit up within. Positive thoughts trigger the neurons in the brain and set up a lightning charge and the mind feels enlightened and calm. This empties the mind of negative thoughts, which have a tendency to weigh the being down. Once the negative thoughts are supplanted with positive thoughts, the uncluttered mind allows light to filter through and the being feels a sense of lightness, as if a burden is removed, and is enlightened.

WAKEFUL, DREAM, SLEEP, AND TURIYA (ENLIGHTENED) STATE

OM is the thought and OM agitates the thoughts. The incessant thoughts churn through the mind in Wakeful state, Dream state, Deep-sleep state and Turiya state.

The Mandukya Upanishad, which is the briefest of the Upanishads, deals exclusively with only these four states which human beings experience. It says:

"This Self has four states of Consciousness,
The first is called Vaishvanara – External, awake state.
Taijasa is the second – the dream state.
Prajna is the third – dreamless, all-knowing state.
Turiya, the fourth is the state of Super Consciousness."

(2–7)

These four states make up the four levels of consciousness the being experiences in its soul's journey. The gross world is experienced in the Waking state; the subtle, psychical plane is experienced in the Dream state; the causal universe is experienced in the Deep sleep state; and the transcendental (a condition where the lesser soul has totally identified with the Supreme Soul) is experienced in the Turiya state. These four states allow the being to experience consciously the different aspects of the universe and Brahman. Each of these states are bound together and linked to one another by experience.

The first three states are experienced by everyone. It is the final state which is the most difficult that eludes beings, which they struggle to discover. It is difficult because it is entirely in the subtle plane, and therefore, needs a highly developed sense of the subtle to experience it.

In the wakeful state, the being is conscious of external objects, enjoys through the world of senses and experiences the gross, worldly plane. This waking state is important because only in this state, the being becomes conscious of the universe around it and of itself in sublime and mundane context, and acquires the desire to know more.

The dream state is where the being becomes conscious of inner-space and internalizes all things seen and experienced in the waking state. This state is also called Taijasa or the illuminated or shining state. From the waking state, the being is drawn into the dream state to withdraw and masticate on things observed and absorbed. While in the wakeful state, the being interacts with the external world, in the dream state, it interacts only with its own mind impressions. Therefore, it is a lonely state.

In both these states, the being is aware of only its own needs and requirements. It has still not become aware of a second party to all the experiences. In every state, there are three aspects to the experience: the actor, the action and the witness. The actor acts out the action and witnesses the action. Who is it who witnesses? It is Brahman and He appears to the being in the third state.

The third state is the dreamless or deep-sleep state. It is called Prajna, or the knowing state. Here, all external cravings have ceased to manifest in a dream, and the being is transported to a state of bliss. It is a time of rejuvenation. In this state, the one who witnesses is the only one conscious of the being's state.

There is a beautiful poem by Khalil Gibran called 'The Madman' reflective of this. It is about the seven selves residing in the body. The poem ponders and reflects deeply about what all is happening to the being while it goes about its business of living, blissfully unaware of the effort being put forth in its behalf.

In the deep-sleep state, the being is unaware of the change in its state of consciousness, unaware that it has ceased to desire and dream. Though the being cannot apprehend the witness in this state, since it has ceased to desire at this point, it has advanced to the next level of light. However, even though the being has ceased to desire momentarily, the potential to do so upon waking is still there, for desires are part of the being, residing in its memory. This is the unmanifested state from which the gross states are manifested, i.e. from non-being, into being. For example, at the instant of waking, the refreshed being states 'I slept very well.' How could the being know that? Because at a deeper level of consciousness, the being knows that it is the same as the knower (witness). The being is able to differentiate between the first two states and this state because, Brahman, the witness, the true actor, leaves a residual feeling within the being at a deeper level. This prods the being to ponder upon the imponderable.

In the first two states, happiness is culled from activity, but in the deep-sleep state, it is culled from inactivity. It is the state in which the being, which has come away from Brahman, resides briefly in Brahman and is in bliss. Deep-sleep state is called the true state of consciousness because in it, the being is truly conscious of the difference between the first two states. It is the beginning of this state which leads to Turiya state. It is the total or infinite bliss state, where differences and varieties disappear totally and only Oneness remains and is perceived.

The Turiya state does not negate or deny the experiences of the other three states, for they are also experienced by Brahman in different guise, for He is the one true witness to the actor and his actions. In the wakeful state Brahman dwells in the eye, in the dream state, in the mind, and in the deep-sleep state, in the lotus of the heart. In that sense, He becomes the actor, action and the witness. There is only Oneness. The Turiya is a state where all doubts about the universe and Brahman, which the being has cogitated upon and become agitated, have cleared. The being becomes blissfully conscious of being and nothing else. It is no longer conscious or unconscious of the universe. It is neither expressing consciousness outward (external world), nor drawn inward (dream state). Unlike the deep sleep state, which is temporary and the potential to wake up to desires is still there, in the Turiya state, the being is consciously conscious of its true nature, i.e., the knower and the known become one. The Yogi, deep in meditation, reaches the state of spiritual consciousness known as Sahashrara. It is supposed to be reached through the thousand petaled lotus situated in the center of the brain. And this is true knowledge: there is no distinction.

It seems an incomprehensible, inconceivable, indescribable state. It is, and it is rarely experienced. In this state, the being develops total peace and experiences infinite bliss, which is associated with basking in the warmth of millions of suns, yet it does not scorch one. The source of this light does not destroy; rather it envelops one in its luminosity. The being becomes conscious of a state of totality, non-dualism, completeness, fullness and harmony.

Om is Water

ACCEPTANCE

Energy starts sweating and melting. The melting heat turns into moisture. The world is made of fire and water with its corresponding heat and moisture. The cooling planets have the potential for water, and thereby, for life. The manifested humming universe has accepted the decree to foster creation.

The 'O' in OM is Omnipotence. It is seen in the rising oceans, gushing rivers, gurgling streams, and endless downpour of rain. It is called Pralaya, literally meaning – chaos, confusion, dissolution, annihilation. At the end of every Kalpa (a day of Brahma), the cycle of nature of cosmos undergoes a change and is destroyed. Out of this destruction, a new creation emerges again. In this cosmic soup of water, (Pralaya Payodhihi - churning of flood waters), God helps creation survive again, and yet again.

"From fervour (warmth) kindled high, Eternal Law and Truth were formed

Thence was produced the night, and thence, the billowy flood of sea arose," it says in the Rig Veda. (x.190.1)

The sound of this churning ocean is OM. This initial process of torrential, incessant rain has been recorded in all scriptures.

In the Matsya Purana and Vishnu Purana (Hindu scriptures), Lord Vishnu takes the form of a fish and directs the first couple Manu (the source word for Man – one with a manah or mind) and Shraddha to build an ark to save the creatures. The same is echoed in 'Noah's ark,' in the stories of Gilgamesh, the Sumerians, Mesopotamians, etc.

This indicates that all species were already present on the planet from the very start. Then, what about the cell formation that science claims was at the start of creation in the waters?

The cell formation is the building block of life and is always there at the start of every Kalpa.

This is described in Aitareya Upanishad simply:

" ...Right from the water He drew forth and shaped a person..." (I – 1 – 3)

According to Hindu scriptures, there are four Yugas called Krita, Treta, Dwapar and Kali. The sum total of these four Yugas is 12,000 Deva years. The break up is as follows:

Krita Yuga	4800 years
Treta Yuga	3600 years
Dwapar Yuga	2400 years
Kali Yuga	1200 years

The years mentioned are Deva years (Demi-god years). In human years, they equal 4,320,000 years, for one Deva year is equal to 360 years of man. The four Yugas together are called Chaturyugas. 1000 Chaturyugas make up one Kalpa, a day of Brahma (i.e., 4,320,000 x 1000 = 43,20,000,000 human years). As a point of reference, this is approximately the age of the Earth given by modern science. At the end of each kalpa, Pralaya (great deluge) starts again. 1000 Kalpas is equal to one Brahma year. At the end of 100 Brahma years, Mahapralaya (the dissolution of entire cosmos) occurs, to start creation all over again.

Today science confirms that approaximately every 12,000 years, there is a shift in the Pole Star due to the precession of Earth (the spinning of the Earth like a top). This causes changes in the weather, which in turn, causes the glaciers to melt, making ocean levels rise. This causes changes in the natural convection in the ocean leading to seasonal anomalies.

Perhaps the 12,000 years of the Yugas also represent actual human years and the conversion to Deva years applies at a larger scale: say, the start of Creation. Therefore, it is quite possible at the start of every 12,000 years for all species to be still there, and the flood story to be true also.

At the start of every Kalpa, however, God's wind stirring the face of the waters can be felt. It is not an ordinary stirring. It is an infinite roar, a roar that crescendos as OM and splinters the atmosphere, and is therefore, called 'Pranava Shabda.' Was it necessary for such a tremendous uproar? Every little process of creation is necessary, for it is a continuous process and helps the building blocks of life. The created universe accepts this and fulfills its potential at a micro-cosmic level through water. Every birth is in water. Every birth comes out making a sound.

In the ocean, in the river, in the mother's womb, life spurts forth in water, and is nurtured and protected by water.

OM IS NATURE

Nature is the breath of God. It is spontaneous self-generation of God's nature. It is 'Prakriti', the created. It gurgles forth in joy, thrives with life and sings forth Om in chaos and harmony.

Chaos and harmony are necessary to keep balance in nature. Nature uses both to its advantage. In nature, there is no moral dilemma. It rains on the good and the wicked alike. The sun shines equally on the good and the bad. An earthquake can destroy the good and the bad. Why is nature devoid of a moral code and seems to punish indiscriminately? If the sun were to shine only on the good and destroy the bad, there will be an imbalance in nature, because the good will thrive and multiply, overcrowding the planet. The morally bound fair nature would be unable to destroy the good and the pure, and this in turn will affect the growth potential of the world. The good, with no fear of competition, will not be challenged, and will stagnate and destroy the very nature that protects them. Therefore, nature, of necessity, has to march to a different tune than the nature of its human creatures, who are morally bound. The punitive nature of nature, where it is totally impartial is what allows life to hum and flourish freely.

The receding waters leave room for lush greenery. The valleys, hills, crevices and mountains are lush with nature in every form. And this nature hums Om incessantly. The gurgling streams, the rustling of trees swaying in the wind, the buzzing bees, the chirping birds, the keening sound of whales and dolphins, the cooing of babies, the mooing of the cows, everything is humming Om.

Every little aspect of nature is a complete universe on its own. It is self-contained, yet, inter-dependent. It has all the aspects of nature within it, and yet, borrows freely and gives freely.

While the seasons indicate a time and place for everything in nature, at a cosmic level, nature lives its existence free of time. Nature at a cosmic level is not just the physical aspects of nature that we observe, but also the invisible certain something within everything – from an atom to a mammoth. It is the nature of a thing. It is different at a visual level, for it seems to separate, yet is identical at a deeper level, for it unites. A rose and a jasmine bloom from the same soil, yet each is different in colour, texture and scent. That is manifested nature. When the blooms wither and join the dust, there is no variation. What allowed them to bloom at the core is the same Vital Force. Therefore, all nature is one and all nature hums the same Om.

PURPOSE

The billowing flood waters bearing the germ of all things created, receded and nature teemed forth chaotically, humming with Om. While seething outwardly and seemingly uncaring of the consequences of its outbursts, nature had hidden meaning and a mysterious method of bringing about harmony. From the tiniest insect to the towering trees, everything marched to a purposeful beat, everything contributing endlessly to a continuous rhythm. It is said that if an instrument was devised to hear the rhythm of nature, and thereby, of the universe, it would be a synchronized beat, and when accelerated, it would be a hum. An experiment done with a mouse's heartbeat revealed that the rate at which it beats (which is faster than that of a human) records a hum.

While the universe is marching towards a purposeful goal, does Brahman likewise have a purpose? As existence and essence, Brahman is Self-sufficient. If the universe projected some desire or purpose of the Brahman, then it would deny God's Self-sufficiency. On the other hand, if it did not project any purpose, and existence did not reveal itself slowly, then, it would augur an uncaring and selfish God playing dice with the universe.

On the one hand you have a very orderly universe arising out of chaos, marching purposefully towards the fulfillment of Brahman's joyous nature, and on the other, there is this extremely chaotic world of quantum physics generated from a world of order.

The chaos is very real, and the orderliness is very real. In between these is a seeming randomness that tends to tilt towards entropy. Entropy is necessary, for it garners concentrated energy for the future. Energy gives way to heat, heat to water, water to heat, heat to energy. Om vibrates through all three, linking them. What this signifies is there is chaos leading to order, order to randomness, randomness to order, and order to chaos, and in this chaos and order is the purpose of the universe.

BIRTH, DEVELOPMENT, MULTIPLICATION, NOURISHMENT AND DISSOLUTION

OM is birth. OM is development. OM is the purpose. OM is marching everywhere. The algae, the bacteria, the cells keep multiplying and dividing in water incessantly. Every multiplying cell generates more birth and every birth is nourished through water.

Ninety percent of the body is made up of water. It is the nourishing agent of the being. It causes the blood to flow vigorously. This blood circulation in the body keeps up the heart rate. It is this rhythm of the heart that pulsates with Om and carries it throughout the body, through every cell, which communicates through electrical impulses called Ohms. It makes the brain function sharply. It nourishes by carrying nutrients and oxygen to the cells in the body. It cushions and protects the organs and joints in the body from the time of conception. And above all, it helps regulate the body temperature by turning energy into perspiration and cooling the body. It helps in the development of the body overall.

In water is the germ of creation, in it and through it, it thrives, and in it, it ultimately dissolves. At the moment of cessation of life, fluid fills the lungs, forcing air to exit.

The water in our body does all this through the power of Om. If you submerge yourself under water, you can hear this Om humming away. A child in the womb is attuned to it, and is therefore, a contented camper. This joy is evident during the initial stages of a baby's development, when there is a secretive smile, a joyous burbling on its lips. This joy is evident in babies of all species. It is said in the scriptures that this is because Brahman or OM is resounding in the baby's ear through the watery womb. The Aittariya Upanishad equates the child to Brahman itself.

"The mother carries the child in her womb
The father bestows loving care
...The child is Atman, their very Self." (II – 1 – 3)

In the same Upanishad, it says, the Sage Vamadeva emerged from his mother's womb fully enlightened. (II – 1 – 5)

Water heightens the frequency of Om and is heard clearly. This is why a whale's keening can be heard three miles away.

Through birth, development, multiplication, nourishment and dissolution, Om is a constant presence. In no element can it be felt more keenly than in water. It is the life-sustaining force of our planet. It is what makes us and our planet unique.

SOUND WAVES UNDER WATER

OM begins as sound. OM becomes space. OM becomes air. OM becomes energy. OM becomes water. All these have sound waves reaching out through vibration.

A seashell gives off the sound of the ocean because that sound wave is trapped in it. The vacuum in a flask gives off the sound of Om because Om is trapped as vibration in its emptiness.

Sound heard above water and below water has a different texture. All this means is that, the loudness varies. If, for example, two stones are hit above water, and then below water in a water tank, the sound heard above water will be louder than that heard below water. The sound heard below water will be slightly muted. But if you put your ear against the water tank, then the sound of hitting stones will be louder below than the one heard above water. This is because sound travels faster and longer under water. Whales and Dolphins are thus able to communicate from miles away under water. An infant in the womb, it is said, can hear sounds more pronounced. It is therefore, prudent to direct good, positive thoughts to the infant in the womb.

Sound waves ripple through water. A simple way to hear this is to hit a tuning fork and dip it in water. It causes ripples in the water and creates waves as the vibration courses through it.

To hear the hum of Om in water, fill a wine glass with water and rub the rim. A hum can be heard. To increase or decrease the frequency, change the level of water. By hitting gently against the rim, a tinkling sound is heard which fades away into a hum.

To prove that sound waves travel through air and water, fill two wineglasses with water. Cover one glass with wax paper and place salt crystals or any light crystals on it. Place the glasses side by side. When the first glass is rubbed, the crystals on top of the second glass will shake with the vibration. If the experiment does not work, adjust the level of water.

Through many such experiments, it can be proven that Om permeates space, air, energy and water and can be heard distinctly at all times.

Water has four qualities: **sound, touch, form and taste.**

Om is Earth

WORKING UNIVERSE

OM reverberated and caused space with just sound. From space came air with sound and touch. From air came energy (Agni) with sound, touch and form. From energy came water with sound, touch, form and taste. From water came Earth with the qualities of sound, touch, form, taste and smell. And with Earth came its creatures with corresponding organs of ears, hands, eyes, mouth and nose. OM had set the working Earth in motion and through it, the universe.

How could the Earth in motion set the universe in motion? The thinking beings pondered and guessed, and pondered again on the mystery of the created universe. Therefore, for the creatures of this Earth, at least, the universe was set in motion with its thinking beings. All this pondering, however, did not stop the working universe. Everything is on the move constantly, continuously. Everything is first one thing and then another. Everything acts according to its nature. The Earth is part of this cosmic nature.

This picture perfect working Earth is part of the whole, and yet unique. Its formation, its geophysical features, its atmosphere, its creatures, are all born of the same star dust, all reverberating with the same Om, yet they are isolated and alone, with incomplete knowledge of the spheres.

Earth, called 'bhuhu' in Sanskrit, is the universe, the globe, the matter, and the subject matter. But more importantly, it is **that which has become**; that which has sprung forth; that which has been born or produced; that which exists. Then there is the second component: **that which preserves**. And finally the third attribute**: that which is joined**.

What this denotes is that the Earth has formed or finally emerged from the watery womb. Then nature enhances it and conditions are ripe for production of its creatures and their nourishment and preservation. Then the third aspect, which has even greater significance, is that the Earth is joined or connected or united. To what is it joined? To the Sun, the Moon, and the other planets.

The Sun, which is a cauldron of energy, has immense pull and could very well have sucked everything in with its power. The two planets closest to the Sun, Mercury and Venus, sustain the maximum impact of the Sun. The planet right behind Earth is Mars – called 'Bhu sutah' – the son of Earth. It is safe to assume that Mars must have been part of the Earth at some point before separating into its own orbit. Beyond Mars is the largest Jovian planet Jupiter, with its many moons. Its gravitational pull is equally strong. So, between the gravitational pull of the Sun and Jupiter, the planets are kept in their places. Of course, the opposing forces of electromagnetic waves and higher and lower nuclear energy also help keep balance.

Mercury and Venus act as a buffer between the Sun and the Earth, and Jupiter acts as a buffer between the Earth and random objects which could slam into it. Thus the Earth seems to have all the right conditions for life to flourish. It is, however, assisted in this endeavor not only by the other planets and the Sun, but also by its moon. The moon's pull causes tides on Earth. It stabilizes the Earth's spin on its axis, which is called obliquity. This obliquity affects the seasonal changes on Earth. Finally, the pull of the moon slows the rate of the Earth's rotation.

What has all this to do with Om? Om is the gravitational pull, Om is the electromagnetic wave, and Om is the nuclear furnace in the Sun, which affects this whole drama. Om is the mysterious dark matter which exerts even greater control on everything. This distinct radioactive hum is the backbone of this universe. The Mandukya Upanishad states clearly:

"The syllable OM, which is the imperishable Brahman, is the universe. Everything that has existed is OM. Whatsoever exists and shall exist hereafter is also OM." (1)

CAUSAL, KARMIC REGULARITY

The working world is humming with OM and everything is following its karmic given pattern. It is the law of cause and effect. Though the creation of the universe was progressive, all the elements in it were needed for survival of creatures – earth, fire, water and air. Empedocles declared that these four are the basis of life and are connected to the four qualities of dry, hot, wet and cold. These in turn generated four humors in the body – blood, phlegm, yellow bile and black bile.

The earth, fire, water and air are the four basic causes of the causal, working universe. However, some causes are direct and some indirect and can be known only through inference.

The earth is the physical cause, the fire is the mechanistic cause, and the water and air are deterministic causes. But for Aristotle these were not enough to explain the causal universe. So, he added the psychical cause, which he felt differentiated the animate from inanimate. What's more important here is it brought the fifth element, space (the realm of ideas), into the picture.

Perhaps nowhere in the universe is the question of the mystery of 'Why' pondered upon more deeply and for so long than here on Earth. What is the cause of all this? OM, Brahman is the cause of all this. How are we to know this? By going back from effect to cause till you are compelled to believe in Brahman, says the Katha Upanishad.

We see the effect of a variety of causes from morning to night. It is the law of Karma. Whatever action you perform, it has a repercussion, a reaction. "As you sow, so shall you reap," says the Bible. If there is smoke, there is fire. If there is rain, there is a cloud. These are visible causes and effects.

Then there is the invisible cause and effect. If there is a cloud, there is vapour in the air. If there is fire, there is energy in the air.

Then there is changed effect. Ice melts and turns into fresh water, which enters the sea, where it turns into vapour, which turns into clouds and comes back as rain. This points to indirect cause, which can be known through inference. Here effect becomes a cause and then an effect, i.e., ice is the first apparent cause, and as fresh water, it is the effect. But as a source for the vapour, fresh water is the cause and vapour is the effect. Vapour condenses and becomes cause and turns into snow (ice) or rain, i.e. effect again. From solid to liquid to gas is a cyclical process and it is ever continuous and ever present.

The direct cause is physical in nature and the indirect cause is subtle in nature. Both causes rest in OM and are instigated by OM and are energized by OM.

For human beings, this karmic world becomes even more important because its law of cause and effect determines their destiny.

Niyatam kuru karma twam karma jyayo hyakarmanaha

"Natural inclination toward occupation and manner of life combined with ability is worthy of performance, and thus becomes one's duty," says the Bhagwad Gita. (3 – 8)

The karmic world brings the being with certain traits and inclinations into this world and places the being in particular circumstances. This points to the duty and action the being is required to perform. And every being in the universe is connected through this karmic world. Each one's action causes a reaction and the chain reaction is endless.

THE SENSES

All our senses are humming OM. Whether it is the sound in the sense of hearing (ears), earth in the sense of touch (hands), space in the sense of seeing (eyes), water in the sense of taste (mouth), or air in the sense of smell (nose), they are all pulsing with OM, with energy. With the help of these senses, we experience life and the karmic world is bound by these senses. The senses are connected to the world of objects. As the senses come into contact with these objects, they develop cravings. These cravings need appeasement, for which the being strives. This striving dictates constant action and reaction.

Since the senses are tuned outward, they are in a constant state of agitation. As long as the craving is not satisfied, the mind is agitated about its craving. Once the craving is satiated, the agitation is about 'what next?' for a momentary lull has come about and the mind is agitated about that dull state.

The senses are connected with pleasure; therefore, they are called sensual pleasures. Since the satiation is only through external objects, the sensation is momentary, and thereafter, yields to pain. This in turn yields to emotions. Emotions churning within always find outward expression through sound, and then, speech. The initial expression, whether it is grief, joy, wonder, fear, curiosity and so on, is always expressed through Om. The mouth starts to open with Ahh! Ha! Oho! Ooh! and ends with 'm' of assent in 'Hmm!'

The senses cling to their pleasure in spite of pain and do not desist from future cravings. This constant craving of the senses is abuzz with Om. Science today has discovered that as the brain is bombarded with information it receives through the tactile nerves, eyes, ears, tongue and nose, the neurons light up with millions of electric impulses humming away madly. Through EEG (Electroencephalograph), the vibrations the brain uses to communicate with itself and the rest of the body is measured.

Whenever the demands of the senses become excessive, the pleasure turns to pain due to lack of fulfillment or over abundance to which the bodily humors react violently. In this pain also Om strums a sad hum.

"The pleasures last but until tomorrow

And they wear out the vital powers of life." Nachiketa says in Katha Upanishad: I.26)

Different from pleasure is joy, which creates a positive hum in the being, creating a sense of well being. This joy spurts forth in the heart of the being through the senses, not in the brain.

"Were the Self existent not there, who could breathe?

He it is who fills every heart with joy."

Says the Taittiriya Upanishad (II, 7.1), not once but many times. In great detail this Upanishad elucidates on the true source and nature of joy. The true source of joy is Brahman, and it categorically states that OM is Brahman, OM is all.

True joy is culled when the eyes perceive a beautiful sunrise, sunset or scenery; when the nose inhales and exhales for the sheer joy of breathing; when the ears are attuned to nature humming away with Om (as in a bird's warbling, a gurgling stream etc.); when the soft touch of a baby gives comfort, and the taste of simple bread nourishes. Unlike sensual pleasures, which vary with the cravings of the individuals, these little joys are the same for everyone. Also, these are unlike sensations, for they do not instigate satiation. There is a sense of bliss in this OM.

Joy through the senses comes without striving. It is enjoyed when the positive nature of the being reacts to the universe in a joyful manner. This breeds a positive charge in the being. The more positive the charge, the lighter the being feels. It is a lightness of being, a state when the being is literally lit inward with OM. The more negative the charge in a being, the heavier the being feels and is dragged down with the weight of living. Joy and lightness are key to survival.

SURVIVAL

OM is the process of survival. What the senses demand is released in the form of energy. The first act of this energy is to appease the craving for food. Food in turn energizes the body, which in turn demands covering from the elements. To this end all creatures expend their energy. While in animals the craving stops here, in humans it extends further. Once the basic need is taken care of, further demands are made upon the Earth. While this may seem needless and frivolous, it is a way of survival for the multiplying millions. Each being has some innate ability, which is used by the others, and thus, all beings are interconnected. This entire process of working to satisfy human craving is an enormous output of energy. If it could only be put together and harnessed, Om can be heard distinctly just like the hum of the machines running in a factory.

It is this difference in capabilities that generates comparisons. It starts off within each species, whereby each individual creature is named and tagged. Then it extends outward to nature, the seas, and the continents. From there it is but a step to the planets, moons and stars. The Earth reveals the visible and sheds light on the invisible aspects of the universe.

"What is this world? The Earth below, the sky above

The air in between, with space connecting them..." says the Taittiriya Upanishad (3.1)

It is this difference enhanced by illumined space and darkness that makes you wonder and ponder and compare. It is the center of our universe, our guiding light. This point of comparison allows creation to develop and achieve its full potential. It causes wonder and excitement and releases Om into the atmosphere in a burst of energy. Taittiriya Upanishad calls it the four-fold vibrations of Bhur (earth), Bhuvah (space), Suvah (the world above) and Maha (sun), understanding of which leads to understanding the Self. A person who becomes aware of this vibration consciously, has high levels of energy. This can be witnessed through a person who is very excited, very energized. You say of such a person, "He is charged with excitement." A veritable energy field envelops that person. If the waves are measured around that person, they would hum with Om, for that vibrating energy is Om. When this energy field is multiplied by collective beings, the potential is limitless. And this is the energy in Om that helps beings survive.

Earth has all the five qualities of the senses – **sound, touch, form, taste and smell.**

LIMITEDNESS

OM is the start of something and the decay of something. It is creation and dissolution. It is limitless and limited. We exist in relation to something else: objects in space, in fact, limitedness. While the collective potential is limitless, individual potential is limited. Even as something is generated, the process of decay has already begun. What has begun in time, ends in time.

The Earth has witnessed and will continue to witness many such beginnings and endings. The decaying process is once again a beginning. It is an opportunity for the young to take the place of old, the supple to take the place of the withered.

This limitedness and decay are a wonderful gift, for it augurs a wonderful new beginning every time. It is but a withdrawal to rejuvenate and start in another guise. Even in this process, energy is used and re-released. The Earth vibrates with it from its core outward. Today geologists are discovering this by studying the ocean floor with its seeming destructive volcanic activity, which generates energy, creating the right atmosphere for earth above; by studying the continuous shifts in the plate tectonics; by the process of mining deep in the caverns of the Earth.

With our limited resources, we are trying to tap the unlimited expanse of the universe. Even though we have entered the space age and have sent Voyager I and II beyond our solar system, and the Cassini spacecraft is even now circling the planet Saturn and mapping out its rings, we are limited in our accomplishments and resources by our finite vision. But this opportunity of getting to know the violent gaseous planets connects us to the rest of the universe in ways unimagined before, opening us to limitless possibilities. It opens a window into the early process of creation, into OM.

The explosive nature of all this activity mimics the process of creation again and again, humming with Om, for all vibration is Om. All this vibration is marching to the tune of time.

Om is Time

TEMPORAL REALITY

All vibration is OM. All vibrations have pattern. OM is the sound of creation. Sound has pattern. Therefore, OM is the design of creation. This design came into the field of time the moment space entered the picture.

When we say time, it does not mean just time on Earth. It implies time at different levels in different galaxies, in different measurements. We base our calculations of everything in space on the basis of our 24 hours days and 365 days year. But at a cosmic level, there are as many clocks ticking away as there are stars and planets. For example, while it takes the Earth 365 days to go around the Sun, it takes Mars 687 ½ earth days, and a Martian day is 24 ½ earth hours. Here we are seeing it in Earth terms. If there had been any beings on Mars, they may perhaps have calculated their year and hour differently.

The heartbeat of the universe, however, beats at a steady pace and keeps to its simple rhythm, which a being's heart reflects. All creatures have the same steady heart beat which is reflective of Om.

We experience everything in space. Experience creates the time factor, i.e., it happens at a moment, nay, a particular moment in time.

Hindu scriptures have used the word 'Maya' while alluding to existence in time. The Sanskrit word 'Maya' literally means magic. If you go deeper – an illusion of magic. An illusion the magician creates using artifice. The word illusion seems to have taken the upper hand and most interpretations have declared the universe to be an illusion, not there at all. Human perception reveals, however, a world very much there. A world which enchants and deludes one, a world which bewilders one, certainly, but a world very much there, nonetheless. If this world is there within space, then time also operates within its confines. Body and mind give credence to this reality.

This body and mind, however, appear for a brief period in time and then disappear. This makes the matter finite, and 'That' into which it disappears, infinite. The finite thus becomes temporal reality, which disappears into the Eternal Infinite Reality, which is Brahman. The finite universe is called 'Ashwatha' tree (fig tree) – literally meaning that which will not last till tomorrow, everchanging and ephemeral. In the Reality 'Brahman' is the unreality of the Ashwatha tree rooted.

"This eternal tree has its root above and its branches below. This pure root is indeed Brahman." (Katha Upanishad: VI.1)

And again in the Bhagwad Gita (XV.1)

Urdhvamulam adhahasakham asvattham prahur avyayam

Meaning, "They speak of the impershable asvatta tree as having its root above and branches below."

Since it is rooted in the cosmic Brahman, it is ever present, and in that sense becomes cosmic reality.

OM IS TRINITY

There are three parts to existence and they all happen through OM. OM, also written as AUM has the potential for being both essence and existence.

'A' is the first part of creation – it is existence and physical – 'Bhur.'

'U' is the second part of creation – it is psychical (subtle) and space – 'Bhuvah.'

'M' is the third part of creation – it is causal and celestial spheres – 'Suvaha.'

To be on a physical plane, the being needs to breathe. To survive in the physical plane and move on to psychical, the being conserves breath. To enter back into celestial spheres, the being lets go of breath. Therefore,

'A' is inspiration (inhalation) of breath and is generated by Brahma (Father).

'U' is cessation (before release) of breath and is governed by Vishnu (Son).

'M' is expiration (dissolution, exhalation) of breath and is governed by Shiva (Holy Spirit).

These three are the waking, dreaming and dreamless state of a being, lived and observed every day. The inhalation represents waking state, the cessation represents the dreaming state and the expiration represents the dreamless state.

AUM is worshipped as trinity in various combinations, which are once again Om. These can be categorized under the following Trinity heads – functions, body, energies, qualities, experience and states.

	A	U	M
Trinity	Brahma	Vishnu	Shiva
Functions:	(Father)	(Son)	(Holy Spirit)
	Srishti	Sthiti	Pralaya
	(Creation)	(Preservation)	(Dissolution)
	Birth	Life	Death
	(Being)	(Becoming)	(Destruction)
	Space	Time	Causation (Timelessness)
Trinity Body	Animal	Human	Divine
	Physical	Subtle (Psychical)	Causal
	Feminine	Masculine	Neuter
Trinity	Intellect	Mind	Egoism
Energy	Prana	Vyana	Udana
	Sun (Light)	Air (Wind)	Fire (Energy)
	Wisdom	Wealth	Power
	(Saraswati)	(Lakshmi)	(Durga)
Trinity	Tamas	Rajas	Sattwa
Qualities	(stupor)	(action)	(tranquillity)
Trinity	Moha	Dukha	Sukha
Experience	(Delusion, Desire)	(Pain)	(Happiness)
Trinity States	Past	Present	Future
	Waking	Dreaming	Dreamlessness
	Sat (Truth, Essence, Existence)	Chit (consciousness)	Anand (Bliss)

Though Om is only one, it runs as a sound current through all these triads and is the support of the whole universe. It is said in the Chandogya Upanishad that even though the rivers flow from different directions, once they join the ocean, they lose their identity, for the oceans of the world form a continuous flow and you know not where one ends and another begins. Just so, all triads may seem separate, but they start out from the same source, are energized from the same source and end up in the same source.

STAGES – AVASTHAS

Time sets the stage. Time differentiates the stages. The triads are woven into these stages, which the universe and its creatures have to go through. In Sanskrit, these are called 'Avasthas' – meaning, a particular stage in life, as well as, that which has to be suffered through, lived through.

The Avasthas are split into 4 quarters or cycles of the world called Yugas:

Krita Yuga - The age of innocence (purity, truth)
Treta Yuga - The age of knowledge
Dwapar Yuga - The age of works (action, duty)
Kali Yuga - The age of darkness

The 4 Yugas are connected to the 4 Yogas:

Krita Yuga - Gyana Yoga (the science of wisdom)
Treta Yuga - Raja Yoga (the science of mind)
Dwapar Yuga - Karma Yoga (the science of deeds)
Kali Yuga - Bhakti Yoga (the science of devotion)

Both Yuga and Yoga literally mean to join together, to yoke. In each Yuga, the corresponding Yoga is in ascendancy and is needed to surmount the problem of falling back into essence. It is the means by which to be absorbed back into essence.

Having said that, while each Yoga is linked to each Yuga, all four Yogas are available to us at any given time, and can be used to attain that level.

These 4 Yogas are connected to the 4 Avasthas of human life:

Gyana Yoga - Balyam (childhood)
Raja Yoga - Koumaram (Youth)
Karma Yoga - Youvanam (Adulthood)
Bhakti Yoga - Varthakam (Old age)

It can be questioned as to why Balyam is connected to Gyana

Yoga and not Varthakam. Gyana Yoga, the Yoga of wisdom is to be perceived only through the innocence of childhood. However, Varthakam is also the time in one's life when one can acquire wisdom. Raja Yoga, the Yoga of knowledge is imparted to youth, who go through the learning period of Brahmacharya. Balyam and Brahmacharyam are inter-connected. Also, karma yoga is part of all four avasthas.

These 4 Avasthas in turn point to the 4 states of human consciousness:

Balyam	-	Physical (childhood)
Koumaram	-	Mental (youth)
Youvanam	-	Emotional (manhood)
Varthakam	-	Spiritual (old age)

These four stages of development are inevitable in the process of the human soul's evolution. These 4 states of human consciousness are linked to the 4 duties human beings fulfill in life:

Physical	-	Brahmacharyam (student)
Mental	-	Grahastashramam (householder)
Emotional	-	Vanaprastham (forest-dweller)
Spiritual	-	Sanyasam (ascetic)

It has to be pointed out that since Balyam (infancy) and Brahmacharyam (student) fall into the physical category, Grahastashramam is pushed into the mental category of Koumaram (youth), even though the householder faces an emotional journey in this state as well as Vanaprastham. It paves the way for Sanyasam.

These 4 duties in turn are helped from 4 sources:

Brahmacharyam	-	Dharma (justice, purity)
Grahastashram	-	Artha (wealth)
Vanaprastham	-	Kama (desires, confusion)
Sanyasam	-	Moksha (salvation)

In this category, Kama applies to both Grahastashram and Vanaprastham. In the Grahastashram, it is in ascendency, in Vanaprastha, it is in the fading stage. The bonds with kith and kin have to be loosened. The children become adults by now, and the being has to accede to the next generation and let go. Hence, some confusion ensues till the being attains some measure of equillibrium.

Moksha (salvation) is returning back to source. From OM the One, everything peaks to four and then becomes one again in essence. The One generates all the above mentioned four states, which take their cue from the triads, which are influenced by happiness and sorrow, pleasure and pain of life, from which humans find relief in One OM.

DUALITY – RELATIVITY

OM hums through pleasure and pain. The cooing sounds of pleasure and the moaning sounds of pain stem from OM. From this pleasure and pain, pairs of opposites emerge. Every aspect of the universe is perceived as a pair of opposites. If there is light, there is darkness. If there is up, there is down. If there is laughter, there are tears. The fact is, there are two sides to the universe, which can be summed up as follows:

Organized	Uncertain
Order	Chaos
Predetermined	Random
Static	Changing
God's will	Free will
Controlled	Helpless
One universe	Many mini universes

Just like everything appears dual in nature, the universe and its Creator also seem to have two sides.

The human mind perceives the inevitable two sides to nature. It is this observance of duality that entraps one. The being feels trapped because while it welcomes pleasure, it shuns pain. While it searches for happiness, it excludes sorrow. It realizes that wisdom lies in reconciling the two. It struggles to achieve this balance.

The human heart has to compromise and find the 'Golden Mean' between the pairs of opposites in accordance with time and place. The 'Golden Mean' according to Aristotle is the point midway between two extremes, both of which are nice. For example, Courage is the mean between recklessness and cowardice. Self-esteem is the mean between conceit and servility. This 'Golden Mean' enables one to live life fruitfully and to operate at the optimum level of human potential.

It is this duality which separates the effect from cause, the created from the Creator. The Creator is perceived as the goal towards which the created strives. This is called 'Dwaita' philosophy in Vedantic school of thought. According to this school of thought, there is a lesser soul (Jivatma), which longs for union with the Superior Soul (Paramatma). The 'Para' in Param denotes the Greatest, the Supreme, That which is most distant. To put it scientifically, the physical atom longs to submerge in the metaphysical atom.

How does it achieve this? By separating and fixating on the fact that there is a difference, then concluding that this difference is relative, for in actuality, there is no difference. The created is the Creator; the created is already submerged in the Creator. It is only a question of realizing it.

Einstein demonstrated this with his theory of Relativity. Time is relative, he said. Here on Earth, in the present when we look at stars and galaxies around us, it is as though we are peering into the past when the universe just formed. To someone observing from a planet on the other end, we would appear to be from the past. This seeming past and present are relative to time. As long as time is perceived, past, present and future are perceived. The moment time disappears, past, present and future are nowhere. An event viewed from two reference frames, explained Einstein, may seem to take place over a billion years in one, and only a day in another.

Therefore, viewed from human point of view, the universe feels like billions of years old, but from Brahman's point of view, there is only that one Eternal moment.

"A thousand days in your eyes are as a day that passes," says Psalm 90:4 in the Bible.

Brahman's perception of time is different from ours, but in actuality, they are one and the same.

BIRTH – REBIRTH, DEATH

OM, time is relative, time sets limitations. Time continues the cycle of birth and rebirth. There is a time to be born. Birth of a soul happens at precisely the time it is meant to be born, not a moment sooner, nor later. The moment birth takes place, death is already writ on this form. What has taken birth has to wither away and perish. We can see the seasons on Earth going through this cycle without fail. We see nature and its creatures taking birth and dying continuously. The dying matter carries within it the seeds and nutrients to nourish future births.

Through time, the fledgling soul travels through many forms before reaching its goal. We observe souls coming into the world at various stages of development. Else there would not be this much variation in the place of birth, state of birth, intelligence level, spiritual level, status in life, health, beauty and power.

This transmigration of souls is linked to the theory of Karma. As you sow, so shall you reap. Every action begets a reaction. At the moment of death, the soul has not had time to expiate all its actions, and hence has to take form again, and yet again to act out the residue.

The birth of a soul is not a short drama here on Earth. This would indicate a meaningless parade of souls, seemingly coming out of nowhere, acting out their fantasies briefly and disappearing again. Much has gone into the soul's sojourn and continues to accrue before atom (Adam) can rest in OM. It is why the nature and character of a soul seem already formed, with all the future potential already beginning to glimmer in an infant. Pythagoras postulated, therefore, that we remember quite a bit from our past lives, which has a bearing on every subsequent life. So, every being is a sum total of the collective knowledge of its past lives. The soul acts out its part in many dimensions. Life here on Earth is but a fraction of the OM as a whole.

The Lord says in the Bhagwad Gita after a detailed description of the universe He has created:

"O Arjuna, what is the need to detail all my glories? Just know that I support this entire universe with a single ray of my boundless glory." (10 – 41)

To comprehend the entire glory of OM, it is necessary to start with the small incessant Om that we breathe and hear every day, which reminds us of our birth- rebirth cycle with every inhalation and exhalation.

Lord Shiva carries all the symbols of life and death upon his person, for He is the Lord of cosmic dance. The half moon adorning his matted locks, represents the birth and rebirth cycle like that of the waxing and waning of moon. The two- sided drum with its beaded wick beats the tick-tick of time incessantly. The skull on his head is death of what has taken birth. Lord Shiva is the Lord of death, dissolution and deliverance. Even in Hebrew, 'Shiva' means death. But it is also life, and it is rejuvenation after death.

The birth of the soul takes place at four levels of consciousness:

1. When it is first born, it is neither holy nor unholy.
2. When it is born again according to its karmas.
3. When its spirituality peaks after many rebirths.
4. When Brahman has been realized.

Death itself is only an experience of the body. The process of release from life is reverse of the way we come. Time releases the physical frame to water, which dissolves into fire, which turns into air, which returns to space, from whence, the pulse points recede in OM. From OM the journey starts again for the soul.

To explain briefly, at death, the corporeal frame becomes heavy and fills up with fluid. The fluid starts to dry up with the heat in the body. When heat is all used up and the body turns cold, the air escapes the form through one of the Chakras into space. In space, air travels as 'spirit of consciousness' towards the Sushumna or central Nadi, wherein, it rests in Om. This central Nadi is the link to the Universal OM.

PROVIDENCE AND FREE WILL

OM, the soul is subject to birth and rebirth. OM, the soul's traits seem to be pre-determined. These traits have a bearing on the reaction of the being to the senses. These reactions are endless and the soul seems to be forever caught in the wheel of karma.

Is the human soul acting on its own, or is someone instigating its actions at all times? Is it providence or free will?

In our daily lives, we seem to be making hundreds of decisions in a day – what to eat, what to wear, where to go, how to work, how to live. We constantly seem to be at crossroads, seemingly making choices. But are we? A plateful of food is in front of us, yet as we try to reach for it, an unseen hand tips the plate over. Only the morsel intended for us seems to go into our mouths. We make decisions about many things in life, but every now and then, events give us a pause. Something beyond our ken thrusts us into sorrow, taking away all choices from us, making us wonder at the futility of it all.

Free will is available to us only up to a point. Events in our lives are preordained according to our previous karmas. Our traits and our innate nature made up of our will and mind, have already been fashioned when we are born.

Sadrisham cheshtate swasyaha prakrutehe gyanavaan api
Prakrutim yanti bhutani nigrahaha kim karishyati

"Man is free only in one direction, and that is the direction of his natural duty, including the learned. What is the point in desisting then?" says Lord Krishna in the Bhagwad Gita. (3 – 33)

The choices we make in this life at any given point are whether we exert our will enough to curb the incessant demands of the mind. How we view these events, how we react to these events is free will. Our attitude to these preordained occurrences determines the future journey of the soul.

All activity the soul is subjected to in a body is a 'hum.' That is, we are a hum (Aham, the 'I' in Sanskrit) with activity, in activity. Whether it's a negative or positive reaction, the charge of electricity lingers on in waves and can change the course of history. Pre-destination provides, free will determines.

DESTINY, LUCK, CHANCE

OM, the cognitive body of the soul, hums through our karmas. Our karmas in every life determine our future destiny. Lady luck has very little to do with it. It is the cycle of deeds and repercussions. The residue from one life to another keeps lingering and it seems a never-ending cycle. Is there an end to this cycle?

As long as man performs his karmas thinking he is master of his destiny in an egotistical way, he will come to grief sooner or later. Such is the irony of man's thinking that when he excels in anything, he takes credit for it, but when he fails, he blames God. The flip side is, from God's point of view, when man does well, the credit goes to God (i.e., it is God as actor and witness who has performed so well), but when man fails, the blame rests squarely on him, for he did not acknowledge the divine. Now, his failures accrue as bad karmas. Is man master of his destiny? Can man be a master of his destiny?

Man is master of his destiny, not in an egotistical way, but in a philosophical way and in a spiritual way. He is in charge as to how he can shape his future destiny. While he may have no control over preordained events in his life, he certainly has control over future events in the journey of his soul. Man is both the most blessed and the damned of all creatures. As a thinking being, conscious of himself and his place in the universe, he is blessed. He is doubly blessed because as this thinking being, he is aware of an Ultimate Cause, and longs to know that Cause, understand It, and blend with It. But he is also damned, for he is tormented by his journey on Earth. Unlike the animals who just live the life they are born to, being true to their nature, man cannot be completely true to his nature, for he is caught between right and wrong, good and evil, mind and will. Animals do not torment themselves about right and wrong, do not fight over the right way to worship God, do not build churches, temples and mosques in an attempt to reach the divine.

Thus, the confused man wonders forever about what chance placed him between this double edged sword: his divine nature and beastly nature. From a cosmic point of view, with such vast spaces all around us, it does seem a waste of space to be the only beings given to wondering about the divine. It does seem as though chance occurrence had a hand in the scheme of things. However, every chance happening is a purposeful link in that very cosmic view. We may yet encounter intelligent beings from other planets. Our scriptures, however, do declare the existence of many such universes where not only highly intelligent godlike beings reside, but who also travel through time warp with great ease.

"There are countless Brahmands like this and every one of them has a Brahma, Vishnu and Shiva," says the Brahmavaivarta Purana.

Man, the gate- keeper of his destiny has no choice but to play the cards he is dealt with. His one chance of escape from the unending cycle of karma and finding that divine connection is to be in harmony within himself and with his surroundings, and thereby, with the universe through OM.

MEMORY

Memories are vibrations stored within the brain. These vibrations hum in the beings through dream, sleep and waking state. The louder the vibration, the closer to the surface the memory is. The softer the vibration, that memory is in the dim recesses of the mind. We know this because the surface memory triggers more emotion than the one in the dim recesses of the mind. However dim the memory may be, even if it is not an active part of the thought process, it plays a part in shaping the being's nature, and thereby, its actions.

Through its journey, the soul takes with it impressions from one life to another. Yagnavalkya tells Udalaka in Chandogya Upanishad:

"The subtle principle of life is the thread upon which this life and the next life and all beings are strung together."

The residue of these impressions can be seen in future thought patterns, but more often than not, in actions.

The arriving souls give a clue to this. An infant is born. Its initial memories are filled with joyous encounter with the divine on another plane. Therefore, it smiles mysteriously, coos and gurgles, as though listening to the tinkling laughter of the divine. The Om from its mother's womb is still echoing within its being and the infant is close to that Om. But as it grows up, the memories of that life start becoming a blur and mingle with new impressions from present life to form new memories. The new memories also resonate with Om, for the brain activity is Om. But the character and texture of Om has undergone a change. Memories of a purely divine nature are now reflected in the physical nature of the being, in its actions. Even though that pure OM is still beating to the tune of time, other mind impressions take a stronghold and it is with great difficulty that the mind can be detached from these memories and brought back to rest in OM.

There are times, however, if the soul has almost reached the end of its journey, its memories can take a divine nature again and retain it through the physical growth. That is why there are one year olds who shine with an inner glow, a three year old can recite the Vedas, and a five year old has knowledge of symphonies and can even produce one. Even when these individuals grow up, these impressions stay with them. Not all the time, however, can the individual know how he knows what he does know. The individual soul's application of these pure memories determines how close to Brahman that soul is.

Memories undergo constant change. Change is in the nature of the being.

CHANGE, CHAOS, IRREGULARITY, SPEED

OM is memory. OM is change and chaos. The constantly changing memories change a being. The constantly changing being changes the universe. How? The being's attitude towards preordained events, its memories, keep shaping future events. These sometimes bring harmony, and sometimes chaos. Where there is harmony, the change is less apparent than where there is chaos. Through chaos change is effected in the universe, and then the change settles into harmony. OM, therefore, generates through chaos and builds on harmony.

The change is first effected at a subtle level, then at a material level. This change reverberates through the universe and OM hums away. Any change in any part of nature has a repercussion on the whole. The fluttering of a butterfly at one end of the Earth causes changes in air currents at the other end. All living things influence one another.

Chaos and change breed irregularity. Every new change brings with it fear and disquiet briefly and then settles down in harmony, at least on the surface. It's just like the ocean currents are never still, the flow and ebb of waves are never still, and every change in tide and current changes the formations of the ocean floor. These formations are as irregular as they are violent. Irregularity is the direct outcome of chaos. On the surface of the ocean, however, everything appears calm.

This change is continuously happening in time. It is speeding towards some unknown goal, with the end never in sight.

Time establishes the speed of things. When you say a car

sped past at 50 miles per hour that calculation is based on the time and distance. The speed at which a thing travels determines the sound of its journey and effects the changes within it. Every speeding object creates a sound as it travels through space. The more chaotic the sound, the more charged the being, the more vulnerable to irregularity and chaos, for empty vessels make the most noise. As a consequence, the effect within is turbulent and disharmonious. Once the speed of the journey slows down, the irregularities vanish, and the beings head towards harmony. The process is like the beginning of time itself. For a more centered human being, one who is enduring, calm, controlled and contented, time slows down, disharmonies vanish, and irregularity gives way to order. Now, the being is filled with OM.

Through chaos, the very first effect took place. Through an enormous sound, OM sent the universe on its course. With speed and irregularity, OM continues to change and brings about regularity in the universe.

Om is Timelessness

UNCHANGEABLE

OM is timeless, unchangeable reality. Time marching by grandly is constantly bringing about change. In the tick-tock of vanishing time, OM reverberates with intent and purpose and leads the being from change towards the Unchangeable Reality, which is Time-less. "Mrityor ma amrutangamaya," is a famous line from the Brihadaranyaka Upanishad, meaning, lead me from death to immortality. OM is the vehicle which leads us to immortality.

OM is the only word capable of taking beings from time to timelessness, for OM is both. Time, which on the surface seems orderly, is chaotic within and keeps effecting change. Order becomes disorder in nature. It yields to timelessness, which seems to indicate lawlessness and randomness and less order on the outside, yet is constant and same ever within. This is the organizing force behind everything from which order arises again.

"Absolute, true and mathematical time of itself, and from its own nature, flows equally without relation to anything external," said Sir Isaac Newton.

This time cares not for change and is very orderly on its own. This time is free flowing and is not bound by seconds, minutes, hours and years. It is ever the same. There is always only that one moment.

The ancient Aryans of the Vedic period believed strongly in the cosmic order pervading the universe, where night followed day, the planets orbited in an orderly fashion around the sun, where conscience subjected men to a moral code, which kept societies bound together. The Old Testament also accepted this natural progression from less order to more order as moving from evening to morning. The Bhagwad Gita describes this as going from manifested state to the unmanifested state at night.

Om is duality and change. The vibration within the womb of the universe causes constant flux. But Om is also non-duality, the One Unchanging order within the chaos. So, there is Changing reality, Unchanging reality, where the non-dual personality lingers on, and an in-between state, which is Steadfast reality.

There are three kinds of beings in this universe according to the Bhagwad Gita: mortal, immortal and unchanging. The personality of all living things is mortal, and therefore, prone to change. What you were yesterday, you are not today. The nature of God (the soul, the essence within) is immortal. It is opposite to mortal, always the same, no flux, no chaos. It is what helps us identify an object. When we observe something, because of an in-built trait in that thing, we say what it is, and having observed its existence, we say it is so (that it exists). For e.g., the heat in fire is its essence, and so we can describe what quality fire has. But in so doing, we also observe the existence of fire and say 'it is fire.' Here we have change (the state of fire and energy keeps changing), and steadfastness (heat which is always the essence of fire).

But beyond these two states is God's personality, where both His essence and existence are one and the same. The essence and existence on their own, however, make up only a fraction of God's whole being. That is, heat as the essence and fire as existence are only a fraction of the whole. God's personality, on the other hand, is infinite and absorbs everything and is beyond our field of knowing, for it is a state where essence and existence are one, cause and effect are one. It is into this vast, unthinkable, incomprehensible Brahman, who used only a spark of His entire energy to create the universe that the essence and existence of fire sink into. Here, both heat and fire lose their identity and simply become Brahman – One.

God is this true primordial, Unchanging Reality, neither dual nor non-dual, perishable nor non-perishable, mortal nor immortal. It is impersonal, uncaused, uncompounded, unaffected, above and beyond place, voice, the five elements, name and guise. Plato described this as the only stable, unshakable reality, for it is not in the process of sliding into something else. It doesn't need to, for it has no beginning nor end, no past, present nor future, no reduction nor accretion. Empirically, we have to believe that one such phenomenon exists. Else the whole universe will be chaos forever, scrunching upon itself, changing from one element to another without having time to form into anything. More importantly, the universe cannot exist without such a stable reality in the background. "The Imperishable is the Real," says the Mundaka Upanishad.

The existence of such a phenomenon can be proven through gravity: The stronger the gravity, the slower the passage of time. Observing clocks stationed in the basement and the attic has proven this. The gravity in a basement is stronger than in the attic, and therefore, the clock in the basement runs slower. From the black hole in the center of our galaxy, to the void in the center of a cluster of galaxies, to the point where a phenomenal Force holds the whole universe together, logic tells us that time would slow down progressively until it comes to an absolute standstill.

According to Einstein's special theory of relativity, when traveling at the speed of light, the mass of an object increases, and time slows down. The speeding object gets heavier because energy of motion is converted into mass. This is what happens to particles in atomic smashers. Mass turns into energy and energy into mass. He concluded that acceleration and mass are the same.

When through acceleration, mass increases, the object seems to be standing still, and hence, time also seems to stand still. We can experience this while traveling in a plane or an elevator. At times, at high speeds, it feels like we are not moving at all, and everything is still.

At the core of every atom, every being, and the universe is OM or Brahman, the imperishable changeless reality. In the Chandogya Upanishad, sage Sandilya advocates meditating on OM or Brahman as the following truths:

> "Thou art imperishable,
> Thou art the changeless Reality,
> Thou art the source of life." (III – 14 – 4)

Becoming conscious of Om and becoming immersed in it causes a lightness of being and time stands still, for the being becomes shrouded in the light. Thus, in Brahman, there is no time, and hence is the one stable reality.

At a human level, a mother gives birth to a complete human being, and yet, remains complete herself. Nothing is lost or accrued at a metaphysical level within her. There is a sense of timelessness in that moment of generation, for she becomes the stable reality for that infant.

The temporal reality of everyday life gives brief glimpses of time standing still, of being present in a moment in time. This awakens the self within to other possibilities beyond time.

The pulsing Om within is aware of this timelessness and is our link to the subtle Ultimate Cause. That is why it vibrates and reminds us constantly to go beyond the state of our own mortality (temporary time) to immortality (no time – timelessness). When there is no time, then there is no change. When there is no change, everything is ever- present, continuous. It is like being in the Garden of Eden, where the creatures do not even know they are different, where God and man are one and the same.

FOUR STATES OF DIVINE CONSCIOUSNESS

There are four eternal states of divine consciousness in the living. The living has been sub-divided into mineral, plant, animal and human. For long there has been doubt whether other than humans, and perhaps animals, there is any level of consciousness in living organisms. All living organisms grow and change. There is continuous action and reaction in them. This can only happen if there is energy within them. It is a known fact that all living cells vibrate with energy. The singular hum within all cells is Om, and Om is a state of consciousness.

If every cell is conscious, then why don't plants and animals ponder upon the mysteries of the universe, the Creator, and the purpose and meaning of life? There is no visible sign whether these living organisms ponder upon the inevitable or not. But within them is an acceptance and a sense of rest, which is visibly missing in human beings. This acceptance and rest are due to the level of consciousness operating in them. In minerals, it is static, in plants, it is subtle, and in animals, it is simple. The process of evolution of the soul through these living organisms is quick. That is why there is no room for complex emotions and cogitation about the universe, which would hold the soul back on its journey. Hence the level of consciousness is static, subtle and simple. The journey of the soul is described thus in a Sufi Writing:

> "From out of the form of mineral I passed
> And as a vegetable lived again;
> From out the vegetable form I died
> And lifted up a head as animal;
> The form of animal I put away
> And took the human shape of Adam – Eve."

The first three states are important, for the soul passes through them before becoming fully cognizant of its surroundings. The soul finally becomes self-conscious in the form of a human being. The Sanskrit word used for human being is 'Maanava' meaning, not new (Maa nava). It points to the long journey the soul has taken. It is on its final leg of the journey, for it has been given an opportunity to realize its true nature – which is timeless, eternal. Om vibrates within a human being's consciousness at a very high level to enable it to realize the Brahman.

> "House after house did God make for Himself,
> Mineral, plant, insect, fish, reptile and bird,
> And mammal too. But yet He was not pleased –
> At last He made Himself the form of Man,
> Wherein He knew Himself, the Self of all.
> And then the Lord of All was satisfied."

This quote from the "Bhagavata Purana" sums up the conscious journey of Om beautifully.

The vibrating Om, which hums softly in mineral, plant and animal, becomes divinely conscious at the optimum level in humans. It is the connecting link between living cells. It is the link between the temporal and the eternal. As the cells die, they are recharged again and again. The vibration within them wants to rest, needs to rest in order to rejuvenate again. Therefore, the living cells vibrating within Om, and with Om are temporal, and yet eternal.

ETERNITY

OM is eternal, ever - present. It has been vibrating for an eternity. Timelessness signifies eternity; therefore, naturally, it is beyond time, beyond the laws of nature, beyond the human condition of sorrow. It is a state where the experiences in time matter little, where all that the being has endured (undergone), moves into the ever enduring.

What we perceive here on Earth within the context of space and time is only a process of acknowledging eternity. Since we are already in a cocoon called Brahman and that Brahman is eternal, we are already in eternity. So, we do not need to seek eternity, only acknowledge it.

The human condition forgets this eternity briefly as it gets mired in the temporal reality of the visible universe. Even though human beings can hear the constant hum of Om at a subconscious level 24 hours a day, conscious awareness of it slips away and the being forgets to acknowledge it.

Plato said that the ultimate aim in life is to penetrate past the surface universe to the core in which the soul already subsists. In this eternal state, the essence of all things subsists beyond universal time. Socrates described this as the nature of something that actually always exists. For example, qualities like beauty, valour, virtue could not be described in physical terms, he said, for physical manifestation doesn't last. These qualities had to be assimilated by delving into their abstract entity. Thus the term 'beauty' in a rose, or a child, or a sunrise, is one and the same and has eternal existence, irrespective of space and time.

This implies that the qualitative aspects of the universe are timeless. It stays at the same moment forever. How is this possible? The force and speed at which the cosmos is spinning through space is so high that it takes only a moment, and that moment is forever. In that moment are contained all the qualitative aspects of the universe. That is why it is said that for God, there is no past or future, only the present, the ever-continuous present moment.

A quote from William Paley, British Theologian and philosopher, describes it thus: "What is eternity?" was asked of a deaf – mute pupil and the beautiful and striking answer was, "It is the lifetime of the Almighty."

God created the universe in one 'kshana' (nano second), and sees everything as happening in that one 'kshana,' and this 'kshana' is ever - present. It is the lifetime of Brahman. When Lord Krishna showed Arjuna His 'Vishwa Rupa' (Universal Form), Arjuna saw the creation and destruction of the universe, the birth and death of beings in a moment.

The clock on Earth runs slower than the clock on the moon because of different gravitational pull. Viewed from Earth's time, the universe is about 15 billion years old. Viewed from the moon, a little less, from elsewhere in the galaxy, much less, and so on, until a point comes beyond space and time into which void the universe sinks and Brahman's moment is all there is.

Visualize a time where you travel beyond the speed of light and reach a point where space and time merge and cease to exist (i.e., time ceases to exist, and therefore, space also ceases to exist), and there is only eternity. Everlasting timelessness, where everything always was, always is, always will be is eternity. And this is God at rest – a state of no change, no manifestation, and no restless energy at work. Everything is pure essence and existence in One. That is why it is said that the closer one gets to Brahman, the faster one loses the perspective of time and realizes timeless eternity. It is like the closer one gets to the sun, the faster the shadow falls off. When this happens, the reverberating Om of the pulsing universe sinks into the un-struck Om of silence. Therefore, eternity is rest.

NARAYANA – THE RESTING PLACE

OM is eternity. Eternity is still and calm. From the surface clamouring of the universe, one reaches this still calm within through OM.

> "If they ask you, what is the sign of your
> Father who is within you?
> Say to them, it is a movement and a rest"

said Jesus, according to the gospel of St. Thomas.

The photons have a mass while in motion and no mass while at rest. The visible universe Brahman created has a mass and movement. The veiled eternal universe, where all is void (no mass) is at rest.

With restless pining, the humans search for that eternal resting place in which they already exist, which is already within them. It is like 'Mriga Trishna' (deer thirst, mirage). The deer has within its womb the cure for its pain, yet it runs madly thirsting for the antidote. In like manner, humans have the Om pulsing within them which can bring about calm and rest, yet they keep thirsting for Narayana.

The center of Om is inertial – where all values remain the same. It is changeless and timeless. It is the state of Narayana. The simple meaning of Nara – ayana is 'man – resting.' Taking it a little further, Narayana can also be perceived as Narasya – ayanaha. Narasya means 'man's. Ayanaha from the word Aayataha literally means 'dependent,' but also 'resting with.' Therefore, while man is dependent on Narayana, man is also resting with Narayana. Narayana is thus man's resting-place.

Where is this Narayana? Here the second meaning of Narayana helps: Nara – ayana, meaning 'man' – abode.' Narayana's abode is within man. Thus, man is in Brahman and Brahman is in man. But while man is caught in the dualities of life and is restless, Brahman is beyond the duality and is at rest.

It is the eternal nature of Brahman, which alone can perceive the changing world of objects, and yet remain unmoved.

"Unmoving, it moves..." it says in the Ishopanishad. If it were not at rest, then nothing can move. For an object to be in motion there has to be an unmoving steady object behind it which moves it. The word unmoved has two connotations. God is the unmoved first object, but He is also unmoved, i.e., untouched by the dual nature of the world. If that were not so, He would be so caught in its plight He would be a confused mass, and so, would be unable to exert control. He is the mover and the moved, but He is also above and beyond that. He is the immovable and unmoved, forever at rest.

SHUNYA, VOID, EMPTINESS

OM is devoid of emptiness and is Shunya. What does that mean? Timeless eternity is restful. It is a place without thing- ness, where nothing exists. It indicates void. However, it is not empty, even though it is a void. There is a different word used for void in Sanskrit. It is called Shunya. It is zero, with no seeming value of its own, yet very important in cosmic configuration. Shunya at core is Absolute non-existence. Why Absolute? Because the Absolute is beyond existence and non-existence and It alone is. As such, Shunya goes beyond emptiness and thing- ness. It is filled with the Uncaused OM or Brahman.

Nothing can come from nothing. Everything has come from something. Therefore, there can never be 'nothing.' Parmenides (Greek Philosopher) declared that if something could come out of nothing that would be tantamount to saying that 'nothing' exists.

The visible universe perceived by the senses, seems full. It seems to have sprung up out of nowhere, out of nothing. Then, parts of it keep ending, leaving emptiness in its wake. A star seemingly full and complete a moment in time explodes and dissipates, leaving behind a void. Then out of nowhere, that void is filled up again. This fullness and nothingness keep playing tricks on the human mind.

The puzzle is easily solved if one can but hear the hum of Om in the void left by a fading star. That is the actual fullness. The fullness of the star that was perceived contained within it no – thing – ness. We can try to hear this Om by pressing our face to a pot with a mouth big enough for our face to fit in. We can hear the hum of Om within the emptiness of the pot. Yet simpler still, hold a flask to your ear; the vacuum within hums Om. Similarly, the vacuum left in space also hums with Om. It is as though all the space out there, with matter or without matter, is enclosed by a huge pot and the void within hums continuously.

"In a pot's emptiness, is its effectiveness," said Lao Tsu.

The seeming emptiness at the core of the universe, a point just before Onkaar rent the universe, where Brahman vibrates with OM, makes the pot called the universe effective.

That is to say, the existent universe is non-existent at a core level. From there, it is but a step to the Self-existent. The existent universe has come out of non-existence (Shunya). The non-existent has come out of the Self-existent Brahman. OM vibrates from Brahman to non-existence to existence and back again.

It is like peeling an onion, layer by layer, till the core is reached, where it is empty. Yet it is something in that core that holds the onion together.

This cycle from start of the universe to where it is today, what it is, and where it is going – all of which is contained in Om – is the point of cogitation for religion and science.

THE FOUR STATES OF THE UNIVERSE

From chaos to order, order to chaos, OM reverberates through the universe. In chaos is the concentration of energy and it causes the Onkaar (Big Bang). From this pinpoint of energy, the Ylem, the cosmic egg, the universe expands and somehow order prevails.

On the one hand, we have increasing evidence of an orderly universe, and on the other, chaotic churning away of star-dust in the cosmos. We have seemingly diminished or wasted amount of energy (entropy) which leads to cold frigid lumps of ice for star, pointing to a frigid end on the one hand, and on the other, there is evidence of recycling of energy and matter, forming new stars. So, while entropy may be evident, astronomers also believe that the amount of matter and energy remain the same in the universe. Then too, if the universe is going to end up as cold matter, with no one orchestrating anything, why is there order now, and who is orchestrating everything?

OM, Brahman is orchestrating everything now. If that is so, then five questions arise which have been pondered upon and answered again and again and in many ways in the Vedic scriptures and Biblical texts and by Greek philosophers like Plato and Aristotle. The questions are:

1. Was the universe always there?
2. Was there a beginning and will it end?
3. Will it simply go on expanding into nothing, or go into cold storage?
4. Will it re-form again?
5. Will it always remain the same and be forever?

"And God said let there be light," it says in 'Genesis'. Did He shed light on what was already there or did He shed light on everything after forming it?

"Manifest, yet hidden, called moving in secret..." it says in Mundaka Upanishad. (II – 2 –1)

If it was manifest, how could it be hidden? The answer from the Rig Veda is:

> "Non-being then existed nor being
> What was concealed? Wherein? In whose protection...
> Darkness at first was by darkness hidden
> It was the earliest seed of thought." (x.129.1-4)

Before the start of the universe, Brahman breathed by His own power. Looking all around, he saw nothing and said 'I am,' which is 'Aham' in Sanskrit. The power of Brahman is 'A Hum.' Even today, when one introduces oneself, one always starts with 'I am' and then says the name. Brahman always comes first.

After uttering 'I am,' Brahman thought to Himself, 'Let me create worlds.' Thus the manifest was an unmanifest thought in Brahman's mind at first. And then:

"Their ray extended light across the darkness," continues the Rig Veda.

Brahman spread luminosity right through it. Therefore, the universe was already there, for Brahman has always been there, and the universe has a beginning, for Brahman shed light on it at a particular moment.

OM is Brahman, and Brahman is OM. Scriptures say the universe started with Onkaar. Brahmand (golden embryo), the cosmic egg literally split in two and rendered the universe asunder, with the vibration 'OM' reverberating in all directions forever. The Brahmand is held together by Brahman as the spokes in a wheel are held together by the center. The universe has sometimes been seen as a 'Yantra.' It is that which supports. It is seen as a geodesic formation of 9 triangles interlaced. From the powerful center, the universe flowed. After that one beginning, the universe proceeded to expand.

'I am indeed this creation, for I emitted all from Myself," Brahman said in Brihadaranyaka Upanishad. (I – IV – 5) The Brahmand is a testimony to God's intellect, and very precise and mathematical in its order. Because of its intellectual nature, the essence of Brahman keeps generating endlessly, spreading farther and farther as new ideas take shape.

Bhumihi aapaha analaha vayu kham mano budhireva cha
Ahankara itiyam me bhinna prakrutihi ashtadha
Apara iyam itaha tu anyaam prakrutim vidhi me paraam
Jeevabhutam mahabaho yayedam dharyate jagat

"Earth, water, fire, air, ether, mind, intellect and ego – this is the eight-fold division of my nature," says the Lord in Bhagwad Gita, and further,

"This is my lower nature... Different from this is my higher nature – the soul, by which the universe is sustained." (7 –4-5)

If we reverse this order, it will be thus: From the Supreme Self, space and ether arose (intellect and ego are reflected in space), from space wind, from wind fire, from fire water, from water earth, from earth food, from food seed (semen), from seed person.

With this two-fold aspect of Brahman's nature, endless expansion started taking place. The universe is always there in Brahman's mind, it has a beginning and it keeps expanding.

The question this generates is, will it go on expanding, the light spread out forever, or will it come to an end?

In this world of ours, we see that what has a beginning definitely has an end. Will the universe also come to an end, existing only in Brahman's mind?

The Shvetasvatara Upanishad reveals:

"And into whom, its end and its beginning
The whole world dissolves – He is God." (IV – 1)

Every atom that has been generated in God also dissolves in God. There is no doubt about that. The moot question here is: "Will the universe dissolve at the same time at some given point in time?"

At the end of every Brahma Kalpa, the Brahmand disintegrates and out of Pralaya, comes a new Brahmand, declare Vedic scriptures. **This indicates an end to the universe, but also a new beginning. So, the question of the universe expanding into nothing or ending in cold storage does not arise**. However, this gives rise to another question? 'Does the entire universe collapse and begin again, or only parts of it (mini universes)?'

"I go forth to make and re-make the Brahmands," said God. In another context, the Brahmavaivarta Purana says: "At the end of every Kalpa, the Brahmand disintegrates and remakes itself. In the midst of all this, Brahma, the Creator, sits sublimely inhaling and exhaling the cosmos through His nostrils!" Every exhalation is the universe waxing, and every inhalation it is waning. Here is a sense of timelessness, where each breath of Brahma is the cosmos coming and going.

This points to a collapsing universe, which will cause a crunch and start the process all over again. Time slips back and forth like a pendulum in this oscillating universe. **The point to notice here is that God goes forth to make and re-make many Brahmands (mini universes), and this happens at the end of every Kalpa.**

Will this process of mini universes generating and dissolving continue forever, or will there be an ultimate end to it all?

Na twevaham jaatta nasam na twam neme janadhipaahaa
Na chaiva na bhavishyamaha sarve vayamataha param

"There never was a time when I, nor you,
nor these princes were not,
nor will there be a time hereafter
when we shall cease to be," says Lord Krishna to a dejected Arjuna in the Bhagwad Gita. (II – 12)

This indicates an eternal, steady state universe. The same has been said in Psalm 148:

"Praise Him ye heaven of heaven
He hath established them (the universe)
Forever and ever..."

Brahman's creation is forever, for He is eternal. Since Brahman has used only a spark off Him to create, there is such an infinite source of energy available that the Brahman can keep on regenerating the universe, or let it go on expanding, or reign it in whenever He wants to.

These same questions have been asked by physicists and astronomers since Galileo, and will continue being asked, more so with the advent of technology. The universe keeps calling to them and mystifying them with many answers. Through modern telescopes and radioscopes, the answers are pouring in. The modern day scientific concepts of the universe as envisioned by Albert Einstein (fixed steady state), Bob Dickey (steady state with a Big Bang), Edwin Hubble (expanding universe), Steven Weinburg (oscillating), and many others are:

1. The steady state universe with two outlooks:
   a) The universe always was this way, always is, always will be.
   b) It started out with a Big Bang and accelerated to where it is today and will remain so forever.
2. The expanding universe with three outlooks:
   a) The universe started out of nothing and it will keep expanding and fade away into nothing when there is no more energy left to hold it.
   b) It came out of Big Bang and can go on expanding forever.
   c) It will end in cold storage.
3. The oscillating universe with two outlooks:
   a) The universe will keep on expanding and contracting to start the process all over again
   b) The oscillation can take place in mini-universes: super novas exploding to form new stars again, leaving the big crunch out of the picture.

Science is as yet unable to reconcile all these theories into one. Of course, there is still much information coming in and many new theories being propounded, and the resolution is still far away.

How do the scriptures reconcile all the states of the universe – the eternal, the steady state, the oscillating and the expanding?

OM is a paradox, wherein is contained an eternal universe; a steady state eternal universe; a continuous universe which dissolves and regenerates itself; a universe with a definite beginning and a definite end at the end of every Kalpa; and finally, a universe held together by a phenomenal force which will not allow it to dissipate or go into cold storage.

The universe is but a thought in Brahman's mind and as such had light shed on it eternally, for Brahman's mind is an ever- illumined mind. At that point, it is manifested forever and is a steady state universe. Within this steady state universe, many mini-universes are born and destroyed, so it is an oscillating universe. The universe undergoes endless modifications and expansion as nature. Nature is the manifestation of God's intellect, and since it is a phenomenal mathematical mind, the changes to it from continuous action and reaction are endless. The projection of these changes to occupy more and more space is endless. The expansion can never end in cold storage, for the energy supply is endless. The entire expanding universe is being held together by the powerful center, which is constantly at rest, timeless and unchanging, and therefore, able to orchestrate order and chaos.

The Lord says in the Bhagwad Gita:

Mattaha parataram na anyat kinchidasti dhananjaya
Mayi sarvamidam protam sutre maniganaahaa iva

"There is nothing whatsoever that is higher than I...All this here is strung on me as a row of gems on a string." (7 – 7)

This is the final answer to all the cogitation. The universe is strung together like gems on a string. The sages saw that the universe was made up of fluid. Science tells us it is hydrogen. The sages saw the fluid as a flow of particles and not actual water or liquid. The flowing particles are strung together like a beaded necklace. It is like the beads that are visible for a moment during a total solar eclipse. The flowing particles are moved by the vibrating OM and are inter-linked. This causes music. It says in the Chandogya Upanishad (I.2-5):

"...Of Sama, the essence is OM, the Udgitha
This is the essence of essences, the highest...
As Rig (Veda) is speech, so prana is song,
And the imperishable OM is the Udgitha."

'Ud' means up or rising and 'Githa' means song. The rising energy 'Udana' raised in song is Udgitha. Prana, the pulsating energy of the universe is music.

There is a string theory postulated by science today, which is the Unifying Principle Einstein was working on towards his later years. Theorists postulate that the whole universe, with every minute atom and particle is humming away as though someone is playing on a violin. The flow of particles in the universe is in constant motion. So, music of the spheres is very much the outlook of the universe. Ordinary matter, even space, time and energy are nothing more than vibrating strings. It is as though everything in the universe is a string and vibrating with a synchronized harmony, and is connected to one another. The second aspect of the string theory is that at the core, the universe is very simple. This very simplicity should make it easy to understand.

The mini-universes, each one independently inflating and deflating, taking from each other are strung out like a branches of a giant tree, all parts of the trunk, yet functioning on their own. This makes possible the eternal expanding (without cold storage), steady state and oscillating universe.

It says in the Mundaka Upanishad:

"As the web issues forth from a spider
And is withdrawn...
So springs the universe
From the Imperishable Brahman" (I – 1 – 7)

Everything ultimately is emitted from Brahman as though out of nothing. Astronomers, observing star formations at the observatories at Palomar, Mt. Wilson, Flagstaff and through Hubble telescope, confirm that recreation of stars is possible, at least on a small scale, as in the Cone Nebula. That entire region is bathed in hydrogen gas emitted by the star named 'S Monocerotis'. A black hole or a binary star steals gas from its neighbour. Hydrogen is the main element in the universe and it rushes in to fill the void left by the fading stars. Thus, an oscillating universe is possible and is happening at a smaller scale.

The universe has remained thus for billions of years. And while expansion is happening, the end is nowhere in sight, neither is cold storage.

Scientists have argued that for such a universe, the Creator is not necessary. On the contrary a Creator is definitely needed. Gravity alone is not enough, for it is the weakest of the forces. Plus it is not gravity alone that keeps stars and planets in their places. Science of course points to three other forces, the electromagnetic waves, the strong and the weak nuclear force, which play their part in keeping the universe in its place. This still does not account for the dark matter out there, nor for the forerunner of the Big Bang, without which source, there is no accounting for the universe. Brahman it is who inhabits the dark matter and is the source of the universe. Brahman is the sun, which keeps the planets in their places. In fact, the nucleus in every atom is a sun, sending its rays outward, yet, drawing the atom to its center.

The sum of mass plus energy of the universe remains unchanged and remains constant. The radioactive hum of OM that pulses through the dark spaces is a powerful phenomenon. The Mandukya Upanishad confirms this:

> "OM, everything is just this word OM...
> Whatever else transcends threefold time
> That too is just OM."

Om is Revelation

ENLIGHTENMENT

OM is revelation. OM is the revealed word. OM is the point before the start of the universe. OM is the universe. OM is sound, space, wind, fire (energy, light), water, earth, time and timelessness. OM is above and beyond this. OM is our connection to the cosmos.

If the spirit is to be at peace, the return to source is a must. The return is not a physical journey, but a mental one. It means getting beyond earthly needs, diffusing the senses and elements, shaking off time and acknowledging the cosmos and its creator through OM. The source needs to be acknowledged. Since the source is already within us, we just need to unveil it to ourselves.

"The kingdom of God is within you," it says in the Bible.

The seeker needs to understand how, i.e., in what manner it is within us. This process has come to be called 'seeking enlightenment.' It is not an easy process.

OM is Brahman, and Brahman is OM. While Brahman may prove elusive, OM is not. It is always within our reach. Through OM, enlightenment is possible. Enlightenment about the oneness of spirit, the oneness of the universe is possible by becoming aware of OM.

OM is the goal. OM is the tool. OM is the path. OM is the process and OM is the result.

Enlightenment is about four aspects of the universe and it's Creator.

1. It is enlightenment about the identical nature of the cosmos and us – **'Tat Twam Asi.'**
2. It is enlightenment about the Oneness of Spirit – **'Ayam Atma Brahma.'**
3. It is enlightenment about the Supreme Power beyond

the starting point of the universe where speculation ends and pure knowledge (wisdom) begins. For this, faith is the key – **'Pragyanam Brahma.'**

4. It is enlightenment that it is possible to experience that Restful Bliss –**'Aham Brahmasmi.'**

These four different aspects of enlightenment are realized through four stages of development of the soul. This development can take place in one life, or it may take the soul many lives to achieve this end.

The Upanishads have many wise things to say about the universe and its Maker. From these, it is possible to put together four different stages from the four Vedas for the seeker of enlightenment.

It starts off with the Sama Veda (Chandogya Upanishad). When the student first approaches the guru (teacher), he is sent off by the guru with the cryptic utterance 'Tat Twam Asi' meaning, 'That art Thou.'

The happy student goes off, blissfully ignorant that he has not comprehended the full import of that cryptic statement. He simply thinks: "Oh good! I am That." Then suddenly it hits him and he stops and thinks to himself: "I am That? What is That? What am I?"

For the second stage, we go to Atharva Veda (Maandukya Upanishad). The student goes back to the guru and asks. The guru smiles and tells him: 'Ayam Atma Brahma' meaning, 'This Self (soul) is Brahman.'

The student is once again happy and walks away thinking: "Oh, it is my soul that is Brahman. My soul is akin to That." However, as he is speculating, slowly it is borne in on him that he is still far from understanding the concept. Sure, the soul within is Brahman. But what is this soul?

For the third stage, we go to Rig Veda (Aitareya Upanishad). The student goes back to the guru and asks. The guru hides a smile and starts to inculcate the student in detail about the universe and its Maker. Through allegory and practice, he discusses the endless possibilities of creation, about control of the senses, about meditation, contemplation, sacrifice, unity, yoga, and ultimately, Sat Chit Anand. And then he imparts the third message: 'Pragyanam Brahma' meaning, 'Pure consciousness is Brahman.'

The student once again goes away feeling he has indeed understood everything. He puts into practice all that the guru has imparted, and at last, like a bolt of lightening, it strikes him that the state of pure consciousness he has achieved has taken him beyond to another realm.

For the fourth stage, we go to Yajur Veda (Brihadaranyaka Upanishad). The enlightened student, tranquil and wise in his new found knowledge utters: "Aham Brahmasmi' meaning 'I am Brahman.'

From being 'That', to thinking his soul is like Brahman, he comes to the realization that he indeed is Brahman at the core. He passes from the knowledge of 'That art Thou' to the realization, 'I am This.' Thus, he finds the kingdom of God within.

Enlightenment leads to that point beyond everything, beyond all visible and invisible space, all that is manifest, all that is known through perception and inference – to AUM, Absolute Universal Manas. Manas is mind. Who has a mind? Manushyaha - man. Therefore man is one who has a Manas, through which he can get enlightened about the Universal Manas.

THAT ART THOU – ONE AND MANY

OM that has been revealed nudges us gently into an awareness of our true nature. What is our true nature? It is not our external nature. The external nature that we exhibit is different from our true nature. The external nature is the outcome of our own idiosyncrasies, our reaction to our circumstances in life, and our desires and demands in life. Such is our external nature that while we are the makers of our own laws and destiny in accordance with our karmas, we are also acting and reacting and interacting with things or creatures of similar and dissimilar nature. However, while each individual nature may seem to perform in isolation, it is being formed by the actions of many. Each individual nature is only a part of the universe; each individual aspect is only one aspect of the Universal Mind. This external nature of all the beings together forms a whole. What is lacking in one is made up by another to form a perfect entity.

This external nature that we talk about is different from the inherent true nature of the being. It is the same in everyone. Our true nature is identical with 'Many', with the universe, with the One. Therefore, That is us and we are That. Here Tat Twam Asi (That art thou) becomes Tatwam asi (Essence is). Everything is one Essence. This first acknowledgment comes because of our consciousness of our surroundings, of our awareness of the Earth and its place in the cosmos.

"Omkaara that is Brahmạn is the Vyashti (individual) and Samashti (cosmic)," says Brahma in Narada Parivrajaka Upanishad. This Brahman, who is both the individual and the cosmos, also has three traits of creation – creative, destructive and belonging to both. So, the created world is Brahman, the destroyed world is also Brahman, and the link between the two is also Brahman. But it goes beyond this. It is not only present in the manifested world, but also in the unseen spirit world. It is both external and internal.

The Bible sums this up beautifully by saying of human beings: "In Him only he lives and Breathes and grows and has his being." The human being is That, and That is in Him, and That causes him to breathe, and grow. There is only One essence. This is **Advaita philosophy**.

The being knows this at one level and knows it not at another level. But the being is aware of a certain something lacking in the external world he perceives and is constantly reaching out into the realm of spirit. The being is caught in this quagmire of not knowing exactly what it is because it is steeped in duality. It sees male and female, good and evil, right and wrong, God and man. It sees two instead of One, it sees many instead of One. This is **Dwaita philosophy**.

When the being ceases to be aware of this duality and realizes male, female and God are one and the same, that is 'Moksha,' (liberation).

Then, there is another stage of this realization. The individual being realizes that the same life current runs within every being, and yet, it is also individual, and loses its sense of self, to become part of the Universal Brahman. This is **Vishishtadwaita philosophy**.

At what levels do Advaita, Dwaita and Vishishtadwaita work?

Advaita works as the **Eternal, static state universe** – where everything is One and the being only needs to become conscious of the One. This is a state where atoms and microcosms make up the whole, there is no difference. **Dwaita** works as the **oscillating universe** where the One caused the other and what came out, goes back and starts again. This is atoms sinking into each other, different, yet alike, merging and losing identity and re-forming again with a different identity. **Vishishta-dwaita** works as the **expanding universe** where the One caused the other and what came out becomes part of the whole, but retains its identity. This is atoms merging together, different, yet alike, and part of the whole.

How does this affect the individual being? Individuals can perceive themselves as One from the point of Advaita, Dwaita and Vishishtadwaita. This poses a problem in the last two states, for if they are different in composition than Brahman, how can they merge into Brahman?

To submerge with Brahman, the soul has to have similar nature as Brahman, it has to be constantly aware of the Oneness of spirit and not be aware of its own individual identity (Advaita). It is like a drop of water loses its identity as it mixes with the ocean. The drop is aware of its identity even as it loses itself in the ocean. It is like the ripples in a pond where a pebble has been thrown. The ripples die and it is as though there is and there has always been only the smooth surface of the pond.

The moment we say 'loses its identity,' it implies a different composition than Brahman. But unlike cannot submerge in like. So, there has to be a similarity too. The soul losing its identity does not really lose its identity but becomes aware of the similar nature and becomes an emancipated soul (Dwaita).

Then there is the pomegranate image where each seed is part of the whole, yet separate. Even after merging back, the soul retains its identity (Vishishtadwaita).

In the last imagery, the soul is still aware of itself as a separate entity, and so, keeps coming back.

In the second imagery, the soul has lost its identity briefly in the Higher Self, which can push it back to life again depending on its karmas. It is like the vapor rising out of ocean heat and the drop forms again.

In the first imagery, there is only One thread running through the universe, and the union there is complete.

This is the state of 'Hamsah.' 'Ham' is the Universal Self devoid of ego and 'Sah' is That identical nature of the universe. 'Sah' also means 'with.' The individual self is always with the Universal Self.

When the student is inculcated in 'That art Thou,' the first step is to identify with the plurality of nature, and then realize the Oneness of nature. 'Hamsah' teaches this Oneness through plurality.

THE SOUL IS BRAHMAN – SEAT OF CONSCIOUSNESS

OM, Brahman is within. Brahman vibrates as Om within. Om is consciousness. Om is awareness of the internal and external universe.

The Hopi Indians declared that initially there was only endless space into which a spark of consciousness was struck. Om struck consciousness into the universe. Om, indeed, is this consciousness. Om it is that changes from Brahman to consciousness to Brahman. Simply put, God first has a thought, an idea. Then He becomes the thought. Then He speaks the thought. The words become expressions of that thought. And only then the idea materializes in the conscious mind of the being.

How does this awareness manifest itself? Through intelligence, thought, mind, understanding, heart, and consciousness, in fact, through 'Chit,' for Chit comprises of all these. This Chit leads to 'Chitatmak,' literally meaning 'Conscious Soul.' Delving deeper, it is becoming conscious of the Pure Spirit (Atma) within.

Where is this soul situated? It is situated within the seat of consciousness. Where is this seat of consciousness? In the brain would be the automatic answer. However, the brain and its activity have very little to do with consciousness. In so far as the brain serves as the receiver for all the messages coming in through the senses, it is part of the consciousness process. It is only the storage unit for information. The thinking activity that stems from this information has more to do with abstract entities like the mind, the heart of the soul (not the organ heart), and discernment (Viveka). Viveka is the ability to link the visible with the invisible. It is this consciousness that carries forward from one life into another, one plane into another.

Since the brain is not the seat of consciousness directly then what is? Physically, it is supposed to be at the still point at the back of the eyes. If you draw a straight line between your ears and a straight line between the center point between your eyes and the back of your head, the junction of the two lines crossing is the seat of consciousness. It is where the pituitary and pineal glands are located. It is called 'Ajna Chakra', the seat of OM. It is also the start of creation. Scientifically this is true. The pituitary gland releases chemicals once every month in time for the female cycle of creation. The chemicals allow one egg to mature and be ready for creation. Mentally, consciousness and ideas stem here, and so, it is the seat of consciousness and the start of creation as well.

If a head is cut up and one searches for this seat of consciousness, one will come up blank, of course. These two glands, considered to be psychical, contain an invisible connection to the realm of spirit.

"A hidden connection is stronger than an obvious one," said Heraclitus.

It is because of this invisible link that the soul is able to interact between the world of spirit and the physical world. It is this consciousness which enables it to cross over from the physical plane in which it temporarily dwells, to the spiritual world of Brahman, which it inhabits, and which inhabits it.

Though it is easy to say consciousness exists and to describe what all it could be, it is still very difficult to cull its true nature and to assess why it functions at such levels in human beings.

It is for this reason that even though the student is taught 'That art Thou' and 'This soul is Brahman,' the doubt ever remains, never fully clarified. The next stage of development becomes necessary for the conscious being. To imbibe some semblance of pure knowledge, revelation discloses some knowledge of the incomprehensible Brahman.

PURE CONSCIOUSNESS IS BRAHMAN – MENTAL PEACE

OM, 'Pragyanam Brahman' - Pure Consciousness, Pure knowledge is Brahman. The 'Pragya' in 'Pragyanam' is awakening, 'Gyan' means knowledge, 'Pragyan' is wisdom. Awakening to wisdom is awakening to Brahman. When through wisdom one becomes conscious of Brahman all the time, the awakened soul rests in Pure Consciousness.

How does one arrive at this Pure Consciousness? Through mental peace. However, it is not easy to achieve this objective. Visible and not visible, comprehensible and incomprehensible, the internal and external universe plays tricks on the human mind. The mind is forever running and churning away with thoughts, never at rest, even in sleep.

When Lord Krishna adjured Arjuna in the Bhagwad Gita:

Naasti budhihi ayuktasya na cha ayuktasya bhavana
Na cha abhaavayataha shantihi ashantasya kutah sukham?

"The Uncontrolled mind
Has no knowledge (that the spirit is present)
Therefore, it does not meditate (concentrate).
Without meditation, there is no peace?
Without peace, where is happiness?" (2-66)

Arjuna cried out in restlessness:

Chanchalam hi manaha Krishna pramathi balavat thridam
Tasyaham nigraham manye vaayoriva sudushkaram

"I know the mind to be most restless
Unsteady, turbulent, strong and stubborn
And not yielding readily to the will.
As well tell me to curb the wind as to
Control this mysterious principle called the mind." (6-34)

Lord Krishna's reply to this is to fill the mind with spiritual teachings according to the character and degree of development of an individual, to keep a constant vigil to attain equilibrium – a life's work, in fact.

What is the starting point to imbibe this spiritual teaching? It is the revealed word OM. It has to be achieved on an individual basis. Even though consciousness of Brahman lingers on from one life to another, it is present in a subtle form and comes to the foreground only through enhancement of internal development in each life, which causes the mind to be at peace.

In like manner, such consciousness cannot be transferred from one generation to another. The wisdom that parents, grandparents, teachers and sages impart can only point to the right path. Their experiences stay with them. The individual's development has to come from within.

Just like the wisdom of others points the individual to true inner peace, the inner peace of an individual points to the world peace.

To know true mental peace, the starting point is Om. This, the sages have revealed at the start of every mantra, which starts with Om. This is getting in touch with our cosmic self.

At the start of this stage of this development, the student should first start off with chanting Om 3, 6 or 12 times in order to cleanse the mind of worldly thoughts and desires. The chanting of Om should be uniform in length and tone and texture. Along with this, control of desires with the help of the discerning and discriminating will is essential towards achieving mental peace, for to a mind which cannot control its desires, peace can never come. If the desires cannot be controlled, then expectations run high, which the world thwarts. Then the world does not make sense, and from there, it is but a step to thinking that everything in life is futile. Such individuals find life incomplete.

Therefore, the individual has to set off on this first ladder by being moderate in his desires and truly accepting of whatever befalls him. This does not mean that the individual doesn't aim for something or looks forward to something. It means that having aimed for something and looked forward to something, if the result is positive, the individual is happy, if it is negative, or is not achieved fully, the individual accepts it and keeps on going with the tide of life, and is still happy. This is the beginning of the mental peace.

CESSATION OF HATRED

OM is the clue to mental peace. When the reverberation of OM within is realized consciously, the individual is complete and full within and doesn't need other paraphernalia in life. The individual is satisfied with what he has and what he gets in life. While he strives for something or the other like everyone else, he doesn't lose his equilibrium if all his goals and desires are not met. He realizes that resisting the negative results of life will only result in anger, hatred and resentment, and true enjoyment of life will be lost. Further, he realizes that anger only causes loss of energy within himself.

Anger with the world and oneself breeds hatred. Hatred breeds fear, and fear breeds disorientation. A disoriented person lacks direction in life and becomes anxious and worried. He gets mired in negativity and becomes negative and cynical. Excess of such feelings causes the energy within to slow down, and the individual starts feeling the burden of life. OM vibrates at a very low level in such individuals and it seems an insurmountable task to rise from the depths of despair and lighten the spirit. The higher the energy level in an individual, the lighter is the spirit.

We are blessed with desires and feelings in life. We seem to have no choice over them. Our innate nature dictates our responses. Where we do have a choice however, is what we do about them, how we react to them by excercising the discriminating will, and how we reflect it through our behavior. Our attitudes are responsible for our mental peace or lack thereof.

We have to strive for mental peace. In this struggle we will be helped a lot if we moderate our desires and demands and accept that we cannot change certain things in life. Unbridled passion and excessive inhibition, neither is conducive to mental peace. Nor does it help in any way in finding the spirit within. The golden mean suggested by Aristotle, the middle path of moderation preached by Buddha is the best.

OM is **self-control**. If we can follow this path of moderation, we can reduce the negative thinking and nurture the positive thinking. The power of positive thinking acts as a force and changes our mental make-up. It helps to control our desires, our outlook of life, our acceptance of life. From thinking the world as a horrid place and life a futile journey, we go to thinking the world a miraculous, mysterious place and life a wonderful journey. Anger, resentment and hatred give way to hope, faith and love.

OM is **love**. Om vibrates as love all the hours of life, in all dimensions. Therefore, when love envelops the individual, he is wrapped in Om. He shines from within and perceives beauty everywhere: beauty of physique, beauty of nature and beauty of spirit. He is ready to embrace the whole universe. He perceives the whole universe as giving.

Om is **charity.** Emulating the universe, the receiving individual turns charitable and so he is ready to give. He doesn't grudge anyone or anything, for he doesn't covet anything anymore. He is happy and contented with everything.

OM is **goodness**. Om vibrates as goodness deep within the spirit. Once it has been tapped into, it is a well that never dries up. When the individual is good, the world is good, the universe is good, his inner spirit is good. The spirit is then filled with compassion. 'Com-passion', meaning suffering together, existing together.

OM is **compassion.** Om vibrates as compassion and stirs the soul of an individual. A man of compassion is loved more than a confident leader. Jesus and Buddha are loved more than the great generals in history. Compassion yields to kindness and kindness to forgiveness. There is nothing another can do that is perceived as harmful. Compassion, kindness and forgiveness lead to better understanding and peace. The peaceful individual feels for the plight of the perpetrator whose soul is struggling for equipoise. Even though the perpetrator has harmful intentions, the peaceful individual is willing to sacrifice himself in the hopes that the perpetrator will perceive the goodness and mend.

Jesus and Gandhi are prime examples of this.

Compassion, Charity and Self-Control are three elements listed in the Brihadaranyaka Upanishad (V.2.3) for mental peace. When the demi-gods, men and asuras (demons) request the Creator (Prajapati) to teach them what is important in life, He utters: "Da, Da and Da." The demi-gods understand it as 'Damayata' which means to be self-controlled. The men understand it as 'Datta' which means to be charitable. The asuras understood it as 'Daya' which means to be compassionate. So, when a being is compassionate, he is raised from the level of being an asura to that of a man. When a being is charitable, he is raised from the level of being a mere mortal to that of a demi-god. When a being is self-controlled, he is raised from the level of being a demi-god to becoming God like. The start of the process is compassion, which leads to charity, which leads to self-control.

Love, goodness, compassion, charity and self-control lead to the ultimate level, which is to realize Brahman through sacrifice. OM is **sacrifice**. Om vibrates as sacrifice within the creative spirit of the being. Brahman sacrificed a part of Himself to create and nurture the universe. The mother sacrifices a part of herself to create and nurture her off spring. Thus by sacrifice is everything wrought. Sacrifice, or rather the willingness to sacrifice oneself leads to the ultimate result of mental peace – 'Joy.'

WELL BEING

OM is joy. Om reverberates within as joy and with joy. It is the well spring of life. A joyous soul lives in harmony within itself and with its surroundings. Harmony with oneself, circumstances and surroundings, keeps the material body well. If the material body is feeling good, the mind is at peace. If the mind is at peace, the spirit is at peace.

The reverse is also true. With the sensitive mind, we have to locate and understand the spirit within. With the help of the spirit, we have to keep the mind at peace. When the mind is at peace, the physical body is at peace. Physical well being in turn helps maintain mental and spiritual well being. With a peaceful mind, we can control the cravings of the senses, and thereby of the body. Whether the mind is at peace and keeps the body well, or the body is well and keeps the mind tuned towards the spirit, either way, the ultimate goal is to reach the spirit and keep it at rest. Very closely entwined are these three principles. Thus we come to a full circle.

The well being of the body, mind and spirit is achieved by being true to oneself. The Delphic oracle: 'Know Thyself,' the emphasis on finding the inner self in Vedantic scriptures, Jesus and Buddha's teaching about knowing the self, Shakespeare's adjunction: 'To thine own self be true' - all these injunctions tell us that through the ages, everyone has come to the same conclusion that to know oneself in the truest sense and to be faithful to this true self is the way to harmony. When you accept who you are, what you are, the way you are in the fullest sense, then nothing can sway you from the path of goodness. To be good to oneself and others releases us from the burden of sin, guilty conscience, fear, worry and anxiety.

To be good to oneself, we always start with the body. We are so deeply entrenched in this physical world we see before us that it is vital to take care of the bodily needs first. To breathe properly, to eat the proper food without indulging, to drink enough water, to sleep as much as the body requires, and to exercise to keep the body fit, takes care of the basic four elements OM occupies: air, fire, water and earth. Air is necessary to breathe, food is necessary to give the body energy (fire), water is necessary to cool the body and cleanse it inside out, sleep and exercise are necessary to vitalize the physique (earthy matter).

Only when these physical needs are met, can the being move to the next element OM occupies – space. Space is the originator of ideas, and therefore, of the mind. In the vast expanses of space, unlimited ideas keep cropping up every minute, seeping into men's minds and awakening new desires. An average human being thinks about 42 thoughts a minute, 2500 an hour, 60,000 a day. How many of these bear fruit? How many are wasted? How many are injurious to self and others? And worse, how many are echoes of previous day's thoughts? Only five percent of the thoughts are used up for daily activities and majority of these are mechanical, to do with the daily grind of the body: eating, sleeping, working, and they are habit forming. A few stray ones here and there urge the mind towards self-discovery, self-accomplishment of goals, self-actualization of capabilities, and self-realization. Of these, a miraculous one gives that insight into the true self. The rest are useless, going back to the thought pile and being scrambled in the wheel of ideas to occur again and again.

It is, therefore, very important to exercise the mind towards proper channels of self-fulfilment, mental nourishment and mental peace. If the mind is restive, the four energies in the body: hot and cold, dry and wet go out of whack. This is why in fear, the palms sweat and become clammy and cold, for the mind has alerted the body about its fears. The cells start vibrating with all kinds of alarming messages. On the other hand, when in stress, the body is deprived of moisture and becomes hot and dry. The mind, therefore, has to be harnessed for physical and mental well being.

When the physique and the mind are in tune with one another, they hear the message pulsating within very clearly. "I am spirit. I am ever – present," OM as SOHAM reiterates 24 hours a day. It witnesses the body's efforts at keeping fit, the mind's attempts to come to terms with itself and achieve mental peace, and it starts to yield the secrets of the spirit. Thus the progress is from body to mind to spirit. The 'Dehatma' (body conscious soul) becomes 'Jivatma' (life conscious soul) and ultimately reaches 'Paramatma' (divine conscious soul). The spirit, which within the lotus of the heart has been drooping downwards, starts turning upwards in joy with the nourishment it gets in the form of physical well being and mental peace. It starts blossoming outwards and the Om within starts vibrating like a bell, like a melodious flute, and urges the mind towards acceptance of the invisible spirit. It is said that when one achieves the true state of mental harmony, one can really hear the clear tones of Om vibrating like a bell or the tinkling of water.

SPIRITUALITY

OM is the eternal pulsating spirit within and without. When spirit is awakened in a being, spirituality sets in. While Om is the physic and the physical cause, the mind and the mental cause, the determining and the working cause of the universe, it is also the connecting link between the world of matter and the world of spirit.

The world of spirit is invisible. To doubt its existence, however, is foolish. Like the air we breathe, it exists like a cloak all around us and within us. Each breath we take is going in along with the spirit. It is both of these that vitalize the organs. But, while the air is essential for the organs to survive, it is the spirit that animates them in the first place. When the spirit is absent, the body is inert. It is the spirit that enables the body and mind to function. It is the spirit that colours the personality. It is the spirit that enables the body and mind to absorb the stages of life. It is the central principle that connects us to everything in the universe. This spirit is 'Jivatma' meaning the 'soul of life.'

The presence of spirit is one thing. To realize its presence is another. It is the highest human achievement. However, since the world of spirit is not visible and is seen and understood imperfectly, it is harder to realize than to harness the mind. While body and mind are connected closely and interact easily, the spirit is waiting patiently in the sidelines to be re-cognized. The body assumes that all is being done for its sake. The mind assumes it is doing everything for its own satiation. Neither is anything being done for the body's sake, nor is the mind doing anything. The flesh has taken shape for the sake of the spirit, and this same spirit is swaying the mind like bamboo shoots in the wind. The body and mind are functioning under the watchful eyes of the spirit. Without this spirit, the being becomes dispirited, and the soul lacks direction. How many times in our lives have we heard someone say that their spirits are low. When the spirit is low, the zest for life is also low. When the being is filled with bodily needs and desires, and the mind is in ascendancy, all three – body, mind and spirit weigh the being down. In contrast to this, when the spirit is in ascendancy (or when the being is filled with spirit), there is a lightness of spirit, a lightness of being. So, it is the spirit that is most essential.

The essence of this philosophy has been brought out beautifully by Khalil Gibran in his poem 'The Seven Selves,' in which the seventh self, the true spirit (the unlimited Self), witnesses everything that the body, mind and desires do. It waits patiently through eternity for the penny to drop, when finally the temporary selves can realize that without that Eternal One, they are nothing, and can do nothing.

When a being realizes that the spirit is present and makes the connection that its purpose on Earth is spiritual even when engaged in physical and mental activity, then it is ready for spirituality. To get absorbed in spirituality, the being seeks tools of wisdom.

EQUIPMENT

OM is the equipment or tool towards enhancing the spirituality within. Om is the motivation. It is the life current that pulses through a being. It is both material and spatial. It is the 'Shabda Brahman' (the word of Brahman), recitation of which links the being with the over soul.

Om is everyone's birth- right. It is vibrating within every molecule in life. But when it vibrates within a conscious body, it is a call to glory. It is a powerful word. Chanting it rhythmically invigorates the being. When a being is equipped with Om, it raises the level of consciousness to the light source. It brings about inner peace, calmness, and tranquillity.

Every mantra begins with Om. It is the shortest and easiest syllable to recite with the Rudraksha beads (Rosary). It can be recited in a crowd or in a silent corner. It can be recited with many, or by oneself. It can be recited aloud or mentally (silently). Therefore, the japa (recitation) of Om has been described as four fold:

1. Performed by the tongue
2. Performed mentally
3. Performed with the heart
4. Performed through Kundalini Shakti (invigorating energy at the nabhi – i.e. the navel).

The easiest way to start reciting Om is by tongue, i.e., aloud. At this stage, extraneous sounds may intrude, but the mind has to rest on the spirit and keep up its recitation, starting with small numbers, and then, increasing the number and time with each sitting.

The second step is to repeat it mentally. At this stage, attention may wander and has to be brought back again and again. Concentrating on the inhalation and exhalation of the breath helps.

The third step is done at the seat of the heart. The essence of the being is in the lotus of the heart. Not the organ heart, but the heart of the being. Where is this heart located? It is situated between the two nipples, just above the abdomen, to the right. An individual instinctively taps this area with his palm when introducing himself. When Om is recited and felt in the lotus of the heart, extraneous sounds start to recede. The being is able to concentrate at this point and realize the potential of Om.

The fourth step is done from the Nabhi onwards, i.e. from the very depths of the being. The Kundalini Shakti (the invigorating energy) stored in the base of the spine rises up through the Sushumna Nadi (also known as Brahma Nadi or the main pulse), and the being is bathed in superior consciousness, aware of only the spirit.

When we utter consonants and individual vowels, only that particular sound vibrates. But when we chant Om, the entire voice box vibrates and thereby, the entire being. The vibration caused by chanting Om creates a bond with the universal vibration. Chanting Om properly (by this is meant a vibrating in perfect accord with the universe, free from friction and agitation) creates a calmness within and without. It is total surrender to the pulse of the universe.

For the Buddhists, the six-syllable mantra of Avalokiteshwara is the tool. It is recited thus:

"Om Manipadme Hum." It means, Om, I am the lotus of the Sound (if 'Mani' is translated as sound). Literally, 'Mani' means a jewel. The jeweled lotus in the heart of Om is the 'I' or the 'Hum', or in Sanskrit, 'Aham' (I am), or, the sound in the lotus of the heart is 'Hum' or 'Om'.

To whom are we self-surrendered? To OM. Through what are we self-surrendered? Through Om. Where is Om situated? It is situated in the lotus of the heart. Even though it hums through our entire being, if it can be located and felt in the lotus of the heart, we can come to know Om as Brahman, the Unknown Principle.

SADHANA (PRACTICE)

OM is Sadhana. It is that state where the being has already started practicing the various methods towards enlightenment. It is a state where goodness has taken over. It is a state where love, purity, piety, justice, indeed 'Dharma' has taken root deeply in the being. It is a state where the being starts experiencing the fullness of life without any hidden motives, without wanting to impose its desires on others. That is, when looking at another, the being ceases to expect anything from the other by way of material things and behaviour, nor does it want the other to conform to its way of thinking and behaving, and does not feel like criticizing the other either. It simply sees the beauty of creation in a contemplative fashion.

This contemplation is the beginning of Yoga. Yoga is from the Sanskrit word 'Yuj' meaning yoke. It joins together the being with Brahman. In the Yogic state, the being has conquered the tendency to conquer others. Instead it desires to conquer itself. The practice of Yoga helps achieve balance of body, breath and mind. Patanjali, who codified the Yoga philosophy thousands of years ago, split Yoga into eight steps, which are as follows:

1. **Yamas :** Five things to abstain from: violence, falsehood, stealing, non-continence and covetousness.
2. **Niyamas :** Five things to observe: purity, contentment, austerity, study and surrender to God.
3. **Asanas :** Postures for physical and mental fitness
4. **Pranayama :** Control of breath
5. **Pratyahara :** Withdrawing the mind from sense objects
6. **Dharana :** Concentrating on an unmoving object
7. **Dhyana :** Meditation
8. **Samadhi :** The individual and the object of concentration become one.

Of these, the first two have already been dealt with in the chapters on mental peace, cessation of hatred, well being and spirituality. The Asanas are many for the aspiring. These Asanas help purify the body and mind in many ways. They help relax the body, strengthen the mind, and in general, generate a feeling of well being. The last five are the means of meditation. Asanas combined with Pranayama increase awareness of inner self and generate balance and calmness of body, mind and spirit. When these have been mastered, the last four stages can be learned and mastered.

MEDITATION

OM is the mantra for meditation. OM, meditate on Soham. Meditation is possible only when some semblance of inner peace has been achieved. This is Pratyahara, withdrawal of the senses. At this point, the being starts to meditate on Soham. Finding a quiet corner, the being inhales 'So' (Brahman) and exhales 'Ham'

(I). This bears fruits in two different ways. With every breath the being discards his egoistic self when he exhales the 'I' and he also reiterates "Brahman am I."

Inhaling the 'So' with the left nostril and exhaling the 'Ham' with the right nostril has a very calming effect on the psyche. This is the crux of Pranayama, the science of breath control. It helps regulate the mind, stabilize the psyche, and results in tranquillity and equilibrium.

If this is difficult, then simpler still is to start by fixing the mind on an object like the lotus, a swan, a chakra (discus), or any beautiful scenery, and meditate upon it. Or half close your eyes and concentrate on the incoming and outgoing breath. This is Dharana.

The being does this unconsciously 21,600 times a day. Learning to do it consciously is the act of meditation. It can be done all day long whatever the individual is doing, as long as it is done with feeling. This is the simplest way to meditate.

Those who have achieved great glory through extreme Sadhana (these are but a few) can reach that transcendental state of consciousness (which is the end result of true meditation). They can raise the Prana to the crown of the head and become unconscious of their surroundings and conscious of Supreme Bliss. But as this is not for all, it is best to start with calming the mind. When the mind is calm, the breath is calm. When the breath is calm, the mind is calm. That is why when one is agitated, and the heart is racing, it is prudent to take deep breaths to calm the agitated mind.

Once the mind is calm, the Yogi can sit in Sidhasana or Sukhasana and hear Om through the right ear. It can be heard by stop-cocking the ear with the thumb. Then do the same with the left, and then, both.

Initially, it will sound like ocean waves, or rain falling, and finally the bell and the conch. This comes with training. Every time the mind wanders away with distracting sounds, it should be brought back and slowly nudged to ignore the extraneous sounds. We do this unconsciously many times during the day when we concentrate intensely on something. At that moment, even if someone calls us, it does not register. With practice, it comes naturally and the sound of Om can be heard even without closing the ears. In time it will be possible to hear the heavenly harmony of Om which plays interminably. This is Dhyana or meditation.

Meditation raises the level of energy. The Sanskrit word 'Tapas' used for meditation also means heat. Heat is generated when one meditates. Conversely, this energy is also calming and is, therefore, blissfully cool. Whether Om is recited or heard, it is beneficial.

Dr. Philip Callahan, who did the experiment on coherent laser energy in Gainesville University, discovered that when Om was repeated in a certain way and his breath touched the infrared spectrometer, his breath started emitting laser light and became a gas laser. As he kept on with his chanting, he started experiencing an altered state of consciousness. This in turn, increased the level of laser light emitted and so on. He concluded that the repeated chanting of Om caused a feed back mechanism.

Om takes those who repeat it in meditation to Brahman. The Taittariya Upanishad adjures:

"OM is the supreme symbol of Brahman...chanting it, the student is united with Brahman." (I.8)

At this point the raised level of consciousness is 'Oordhvamukha', i.e., face (vision) turned upward. This is the state of Omkaara, where the subject and object become a single point of energy as when creation took place. This is Samadhi, when the individual and the object become one.

PRAYER

OM is meditation. Om is repetition. Om is invocation. In today's fast paced life, where it is difficult to find peaceful corners to meditate, prayer is the instinctive alternative. Even if we cannot gain complete, absolute knowledge of Brahman, we can certainly feel connected to it through prayer.

Lord Krishna says in the Bhagwad Gita: "Uttering the one syllabled Om that denotes Brahman, the Yogi who, thinking of Me, departs from this body, attains the Supreme Goal." (8-3-5)

Even if one cannot achieve the status of a Yogi, if one can fix one's thoughts on Om and seeing Brahman in everything, ascribe every action to It, then one reaches Brahman.

The Lord Himself seems to realize that not all beings are able to attain perfection. One in a million does so, and even he has imperfect knowledge of Brahman. Therefore, the Lord classifies those who pray to Him under four heads:

1. The Aarta (distressed)
2. The Jigyasu (curious, enquiring)
3. The Artharthi (desirous of wealth)
4. The Gyani (wise)

These four can be further classified under:

1. Prayers of need and plead – That is the way the distressed pray.
2. Prayers of query and understanding – That is the way the curious pray.
3. Prayers of greed and want – That is the way the desirous pray.
4. Prayers of Praise and meditative silence – That is the way the wise pray.

Ninety five percent of the world's population believes in God and at some time or the other is engaged in prayer. Even the agnostic and the atheist is drawn to prayer in times of distress, even if it is only to insult God. Whether one believes in a Creator or not, a Creator who has control over our destiny or a Creator who is helpless, the instinct to plead and pray is within us. Whether one believes in a Creator or not, Om is a reality that cannot be ignored. Both scriptures and science declare this background hum of the universe to be true. The Om within us keeps reminding us of our connection to Brahman all day and night.

Prayer is a vital part of a conscious being. When you pray, the external spirit gets centered within. The healing process that takes place results in equilibrium. The beat of the heart steadies to the same rate as the pulse of the universe and allows you to re-charge your being with the universal energy Om.

I AM BRAHMAN – SALVATION

OM is Brahman. The intangible spirit within is Brahman. The being is Brahman in its purest form. Om is salvation. Yoga, practice of meditation and prayer yields the desired results. The being becomes aware of Brahman. Knowledge of Brahman saturates the calm mind.

It is a peculiar state, for scriptures stress that true and complete knowledge of Brahman is impossible. Then what exactly does the being realize and see as Brahman? Kena Upanishad sheds light on this. If a being says that he knows Brahman fully, then he assuredly knows him not. On the other hand: "He amongst us who understands the spirit of the words, and says 'Nor do I know that I know him not,'" really knows Brahman. What this signifies is, exact knowledge of Brahman is beyond human capacity. But there is some inkling of Brahman to be garnered through practice of yoga, meditation and prayer, for Brahman provokes this fascination with Him from within. So, when a being says 'Aham Brahmasmi' (I am Brahman), he is right and he is not so right.

This piece of wisdom has been summed in Jain philosophy beautifully, according to which, the Jiva (being) is Atman in bondage, and the Atman (Brahman) is Jiva liberated. What this means is, within the Jiva, the Atman (Brahman) resides and he is in bondage, for the Jiva realizes not his presence. And because Atman resides within the Jiva, and the Atman is ever free, the Jiva is ever liberated. This could be taken one step further. The Jiva resides in a cocoon called Atman, which is ever free. Therefore, when the Jiva re-cognizes the unfettered Atman, it is liberated. So, bondage and liberation are ever present in a being. To realize this is to know Brahman.

The being realizes he is not separate from Brahman. The spirit within is the same as Brahman, has been the same since the start of time, and it is eternal. The soul of the being becomes purified at this point. Purified of what? Purified of the worldly burden. It begins to see the play of the world as just play. It sees itself as this beautiful light which has neither beginning nor end. This bliss is inexplicable and there is nothing beyond it. Having achieved this status, it continues with life, unshaken by whatever it throws. This is salvation, where the soul is saved from the torment of living, for even in that state, it is sees only Brahman (i.e., becomes God conscious) and is therefore, Brahman.

Salvation, which is freedom to experience life at its fullest, creates perfection. Such perfection does not mean that the duality of life is no longer present. It means that the pair of opposites, the competing and complimentary forces of life are seen as perfect in their own way, every one of them acting according to their own inner traits even as Brahman intended. Variety is Brahman, and underneath this variety is one thread connecting everything. At this point the being perceives the universal in every form and begins to comprehend the Unifying Universal Spirit of OM where the vibration in a cat, a dog and man become one, there is no distinction, and everything is perfect. Since Brahman created everything, and Brahman is perfect, everything is perfect. This is the Ultimate Truth.

SAT CHIT ANAND

OM is Truth (Essence). OM is consciousness (Existence, Presence). OM is bliss (Both here and beyond). It is Sat (Truth) Chit (Consciousness) Anand (Bliss). The enlightened being arrives at this stage and realizes what a tremendous journey its soul has undertaken. From perceiving the world as unreal, temporal, it has gone on to see it as very real, eternal and true. This is 'Viveka' (wisdom) where the being can differentiate between the visible world and the invisible spirit world and sees the connection between the two clearly.

Truth is Brahman, the very basis of existence. 'Sat' also means essence. The being sees this essence of Brahman reflected in everything, for without this essence, there is no existence. Realizing this, the being becomes conscious. This is not the ordinary, day-to-day consciousness all creatures are subject to. This is not the consciousness human beings experience. It is the consciousness of the awakened being. The 'Chit' (the 'chi' of oriental philosophy) has withdrawn from the visible and gone to the invisible, and reached that glorious plane where Brahman alone is. 'OM Tat Sat'. OM is equivalent to That and That is the Truth. And Truth is existence. This is totality of existence. This is coming from the Absolute Spiritual plane to the external physical plane, and going back from the physical plane to the internal spiritual plane. All is seen in a moment. It is what a day of Brahman is like. With the dawn of its day, existence comes into being, and with its night comes the dissolution of existence. This is proclaimed by Lord Krishna in the Bhagwad Gita (8–18):

Avyaktaat vyaktyaha sarvaaha prabhavanti aharagame
Ratryagame praliyante tatra eva avyaktasangyake

"With the coming of the day (Brahma's), all the manifest forms proceed from the unmanifest,

With the coming of the night all this enters the state of dissolution known as the unmanifest."

This happens every moment for Brahman, for whom the entire cosmic period is but a moment.

When the awakened being becomes conscious of Brahman or pure existence alone, then it experiences 'Anand'. It has no worry, no anxiety, no fear, and no hatred. It is basking in the Holy Spirit. It is blissfully conscious of simply - being.

Sat is the father, Chit is the son, and Anand is the Holy Spirit. Sat is Brahma, Chit is Vishnu (who takes incarnations so that the beings may become conscious of Him), and Anand is Shiva, the Holy Spirit.

SHIVOM

Shivom or Shivam is OM. Om is in Shivom. It is the final expression of God's blessings. Truth is Shiva (Satyam), Auspiciousness is Shiva (Shivam), and Beauty is Shiva (Sunderam). Shiva is, therefore, the ultimate expression of beatitude.

Shivom, Shalom is peace. But then Shiva is also the power of dissolution. Even in Hebrew, Shiva means death. Then how can Shiva represent peace? Shiva is the Holy Spirit. He is the Lord of Omkaara, called Omkaarnath (also spelt Onkaarnath). He is terrible in Pralaya (destructive) form, but he is gentle in Moksha (liberation). He brings ultimate peace to a being. Therefore, Shivom is peace.

In the light of the Holy Spirit, we can experience all bliss, pure bliss. It is the ultimate light source. It is the ultimate Truth, Beauty and Love. In that Love, we can bask forever. When we bask in that light, the agitation of the mind ceases.

Shiva is also represented as 'Ardhanarishwara' – i.e., as half male and half female. The male is Shiva and the female is Parvati. Shiva represents 'Vak' (word) and Parvati 'Artha' (form). In another sense, word indicates light energy and form indicates sound energy. However, Parvati is also called 'Shakti', which is pure energy, and in that instance, Shiva becomes matter. Then, their son Skanda becomes light energy and Ganesha, sound energy. The thing to note is everything stems from Shiva.

Shiva is the Absolute Entity. Since the Absolute Entity is beyond comprehension. It remains in essence nameless and formless. So, the Shiva Purana disclosed an abstract entity that has neither form nor name to be worshipped in this world. It is called 'Lingam'. More realistically, all forms and all names can be ascribed to it. 'Lingam' means, that which symbolizes. The popular belief is that the Lingam is a phallic symbol and as such, it is the symbol of creation. This is at a very earthy, material level. Linga is from the Sanskrit word 'Li' which implies 'Leeyathe', meaning to merge. It is the form into which everything else merges. In Vedantic philosophy, it is the indestructible subtle, original frame or cause. The twelve aspects of Lingams described in the purana include the five elements, the Superior Soul, the Light with bliss, the sun, moon and fire, the Causeless Lord of the Universe, and time with death.

The Lingam is shaped more like a cylinder than a phallus. The ancient domes of Cathedrals and mosques, the modern domes of Parliament houses and sports arenas, the domes of temples in North India, the domes of observatories at Mauna K, Palomar and other places are all in the shape of a Linga. The cavity within these domes resonates with Om. Try uttering Om under these domes, and it will reverberate and come back to you, enhancing your Chit.

Lingam has been described as a cylindrical darkness, which stretches from end to end and spans the entire universe. It is dark, though it generates all the colors of life. It is so powerful it holds the universe together. Therefore, it is the center of the universe and the entire expanse of the universe. It represents no particular shape, yet all shapes are contained in it.

The foremost Linga is devoid of smell, taste, colour, hearing and touch and is known as pure Prakriti (pure nature).

Linga is one. It is the symbol of the start of space and time, and it is the symbol where space and time disintegrate and meet singularity.

The black hole which scientists are trying to find has been defined as this dense collapsed star, whose gravitational pull has become so strong that it attracts everything towards it and absorbs it. Because it is so dense, no light can escape it. Though, as yet, there are no pictures of it but only radiosignals to declare its presence, scientists have come to the conclusion that of necessity, because they see gases from other stars and planets pulled towards some source, that that source is a black hole.

Because it is a black hole, they can never capture its image. Further, if an object or a person were to head towards the black hole and enter it, gravity will stretch and distort the thing so much that it will disintegrate into nothingness. On the other hand, if the black hole is not so powerful but a moderate one, then it is possible that the object can travel away from the source of light at the top of the black hole and go through it, ultimately meeting the point of singularity and pop into the other side of Big Bang.

The nucleus of the universe is Brahman, whose radiant effulgence (Bhargo) is the singularity. So, while you are drawn inexorably towards the center called Brahman, you would not be destroyed or distorted. If you are lucky enough, you would be bathed in the effulgence of Brahman and experience singularity. Once merged with singularity, the being loses its identity and does not come out to tell of it. Or does it? We have sages and seers, messiahs like Jesus, enlightened beings like Buddha, who return (metaphysically) to earth after losing themselves in that light, to tell us about the glory of that singularity.

This theory, astrophysicist, Stephen Hawking, has pondered upon and presented, as recently as July 2004, at the International Conference on General Relativity and Gravitation. He has backed off on his own theories wherein he had stated that nothing can come out of the black hole to say that it is possible for things to emerge back from a black hole and give us clues to the universe.

The tunnel connecting the two sides of the Big Bang has been termed a worm- hole. In modern scientific terms, the wormhole can be seen as an example of a Lingam. The worm-hole, which is an invisible tunnel between two black holes, or a connection to galaxies, or two dimensions of the universe, has been described in the Puranas as the invisible travel path between worlds. It has been postulated that if these wormholes exist then it would take less than an hour to travel between two worlds. Rishis traveled from one Brahmand to another in a matter of hours and minutes. Sage Narada is seen going from Shivaloka to Brahmaloka to Vaikunta (Vishn's abode) in the blink of an eyelid.

Whether we call it wormhole, or invisible tunnel, or Lingam, it is the connection between existence and non-existence, between the manifest and unmanifest, between matter and emptiness.

Lao Tzu has described this succinctly in the 'Book of meaning and life':

"Doors and windows are cut in the walls of a house,
And because they are empty, we are able to use them.
Therefore, on the one hand we have the
Benefit of existence, and on the other,
We make use of non-existence."

Meditating upon the known heard Om, leads to the Unknown Absolute Truth – Shivom, which is non-existence. In non-existence is contained singularity.

Om is Singularity

NON EXISTENCE – UNMOVING PRINCIPLE

OM is non-existence. The moment we say non-existence, it indicates that nothing exists. This, however, is not true. The One exists. This is the Absolute Truth. Since OM exists as Gunas (qualities), as a formless, timeless, spaceless, causeless, changeless, beginningless Reality, it seems feasible to say, it is non-existence. It is 'Less' or devoid of the qualitative and quantitative. It is the One that makes it possible for quality to exist in quantity. For example, it exists as liquid in water, vapour in gas, and solid in ice. It is one and the same thing, but it is OM or Brahman's essence that gives rise to the specific quality in a thing. LaoTzu said in 'The book of Meaning and Life':

"All this has been effected by the One.
If Heaven were not pure through it, it would have to burst.
If Earth were not firm through it, it would have to falter...
If things had not come into existence through it,
They would have to perish."

It is the One that creates, preserves and dissolves. It is 'trigunatmak' (three qualities) in one.

Without this Reality, the existent cannot exist, breathe and survive. This Reality is within the universe and outside it. Scientists call this anti-matter.

"As the essence of the world, God enfoldeth the world, but at the same time, He is also in our midst and even in our own bodies," said Na Kae Taju, the Japanese philosopher.

Not only is It within and without, It is also moving and unmoving, known, and yet, unknown. "This Self is One – Unmoving it outruns pursuit," declared the Ishopanishad, and further elucidated,

"Unmoving, it moves - is far away, yet near, within all, outside all. Out of Self comes the breath that is the life of all things." (4 – 5)

This unmoving principle, which is beyond pursuit, elusive to knowledge, is yet within our grasp as the vital energy Om. It enters the being as Jiva Shakti (life giving energy) through the head. It joins Prana or the vital energy (located at the base of the spine) to make the being function. This is why the bone marrow is so crucial to survival.

Since the Jiva Shakti is the same in everyone, it is called 'Chit Shakti'. Chit Shakti is the universal energy. Many physicists believe that in the beginning was a single point with a single force. This single force became many, and many became difficult to grasp. Human brain is not sufficient to grasp the intricate universe at the same time, but it can grasp the One. God is simplicity itself, the universe is complexity itself. The source of the universe is most simple. Singularity is simple. It is just the One. It is easy to understand the One. Many are difficult. Comprehending the One source will open the door to many. It makes everything exist. Take it away and we die, even though the earth, water, air, fire, space, time and consciousness are still all around us. The universal energy energizes every cell in the universe. The physical sheath, consciousness, mind, will, breath are all at its mercy, for they are all temporal and subject to change. But the universal energy is constant, unchanging and the same in everything, whether the object is big or small.

Astronomers have made a fundamental tenet that the Milky Way galaxy is not unique or different from other galaxies. They call this the cosmological principle, which is that the universe must be the same everywhere and in all directions. If this were not so, then there would be no uniformity of nature, i.e., the laws of physics applicable here on earth would not be applicable to the rest of the universe.

Charles Siebert of the New York Time said: "The Buddhists spoke of the life force running through all things. What is the current understanding of DNA as the common substrate of all existence but a verification of that idea?"

This common substrate runs through everything, links everything, and unites everything as one. So, while the mind personalities are many, souls are many, the life running through everything is One. Call it Vital Energy, Universal Energy, Life Force, Absolute Truth or Non-Existence, it is the same power. The Upanishads, after calling it the Self, Supreme Self, Atman etc., ultimately called it Brahman. They further classified it as the silent substratum of the universe. Therefore, at the core, life is silence. Even though it is pulsating and vibrating with the power of the Absolute, it is still silent – Anahat. Out of this silence, word arises, and this word is OM. OM vibrates, reverberates and disintegrates within every cell in the universe. Put another way, the three-fold task of Brahman is creation, preservation and dissolution. To this is added a fourth dimension, which is 'Absorption' or Om. Through Om, it is possible to not just dissolve but get absorbed back into the silence from which we arose.

Everything in the universe is Om. Everything in the universe is Brahman. Everything in the universe vibrates with Om and worships Om. Everything in the universe is the same on the inside. Everything in the universe seems different on the outside. Since outside differences are still part of the same Brahman, everything outside is also the same. The arms, legs, torso, neck and head are separate yet part of a whole. They seem different, but are made up of the same bone, blood and flesh and every cell pulsates with the same Om. So it is with the separate entities in the universe. More importantly, everything in the universe can slide from one thing into another, from one form of energy into another, and thus, once again, is the same outside. This is the Absolute Universal Truth.

RADIANT ENERGY

OM is radiant energy. Every cell radiates this Om. Every object in the universe emits the same radiant energy. Then why are we unable to see this radiant energy? It is because some are visible and some are not. The sun, for example, emits radiant energy at a very high frequency because of its high temperature. Therefore, it is visible. The Earth also emits this radiant energy. But since it is much cooler, it has a lower frequency than that of the sun, and therefore, visible only through infrared waves.

The coolness or high temperature determines the frequency of objects. Objects may vibrate at low or high frequencies, but vibrate they do. This vibrating hum in everything is Om and it emits forth as radiant energy.

The essence of this radiant energy is the same in everything whether one believes in **Advaita** (Brahman and nature are uniform), **Dwaita** (Duality – Brahman and Prakriti or nature become separate and then merge), or **Vishishtadwaita** (Brahman and nature are distinguished, yet identical entities and retain identity even after merging).

Through oneness, duality and identical nature, runs only one thing. Thales, one of the very first philosophers, realized that the material world could be subdivided and reduced to a single element. He assumed this one thing common to all objects to be water. Water was the common assumption made by many, especially since it is the womb of life, and hydrogen is the major gas girdling the universe.

What Thales missed was that the single element could be subdivided further and further until it could no longer be done or nothing remained. Today science has discovered that the atom becomes part less and no longer knowable and classifiable. Physicist, Murray Gell-Mann found a way to break down the protons in an atom and discovered 'Quarks'. From the 'Quark' stage, if anything is to be known about the atom, it has to be through inference.

This fact the Mundaka Upanishad (I – 1 – 6) declared thus: "Because the Self is a fine substance, It slips from the mind and deludes imagination."

The only clue we have to this fine substance is as the life current flowing within us. It is like the same current that runs through bulbs. The shapes and sizes may be different, but the light in them is the same. OM, the oneness of Brahman goes further. It is the current and the bulb and the shape. The light, the warmth and the source are one and the same, just like the mind, the will and the soul are all distinct, yet, part of the same.

The radiant energy is experienced as Om consciousness in beings. The consciousness of beings, though seemingly plural, is in actuality, only one. The multiplicity is only apparent at a physical level. Consciousness, therefore, is never experienced in the plural, but only in the singular.

A German translation by Fritz Meyer of the 13th century mystic Aziz Nasafi's work sums this up beautifully:

"On the death of any living creature, the spirit returns to the spiritual world, the body to the bodily world. In this however only the bodies are subject to change. The spiritual world is one singular spirit who stands like unto a light behind the bodily world and who, when any single creature comes into being, shines through it as through a window. According to the kind and size of the window less or more light enters the world. The light itself however remains unchanged."

Sir J.A. Thomson said, "...There is from the amoeba upwards, a stream of inner, of subjective life, it may be only a slender rill, but sometimes it is a strong current."

This current is so radiant that it can engulf us in its warmth and not harm us. The Upanishads say we feel a magical state of Bliss in its presence. This is easy to verify by holding a sparkler in hand. Even though the center burns at 2000°, the sparks flying off do not harm us.

Many people who have had near death experiences describe being in the presence of or being touched by an extraordinary white light, which is so great in intensity, yet envelopes them in its cool warmth. The magnetic pull of Brahman is supposed to be at a very high frequency, and hence, harmless. On the contrary, it is greatly beneficial, for fear of life goes away and an appreciation of life takes over. This is because the radiant energy is benign Effulgence of Brahman. It is the life current of the universe. This life current sets action in motion. Every action has a reaction. Every action vibrates with Om, and every reaction reverberates with Om. The interaction between action and reaction resonates with Om until there is nothing between them but OM. It is the very pulse of life and it is singular in nature.

OM TAT SAT

OM is the beginning. OM is Tat (That). OM is Sat (Truth).

The first manifestation of That Truth took form as the unspoken syllable Om (Anahat – the silence underlying the universe). Om is not a sound emanated from Brahman, but

Brahman vibrating from within. It existed as non-being first. That is, it existed as a thought in Brahman's mind, and therefore, it was not in a state of being. From this non-being, came, being (substance, existence).

The being then strives to achieve the state of non-being as it is in effect non-being, for it owes its existence to the mind of that Supreme Being. From this state of non-being it has to go back to simply being.

Non-being to being, being to non-being, it is as though a role reversal is taking place. First Brahman is the non-being and we the being. Then we turn into non-being and Brahman becomes The Being (The only One that exists).

This is Tat, That or the essence, or the essential nature or fact. It is important to realize this underlying essence in everything as belonging to the Uncaused One, especially for those seeking liberation, enlightenment, and knowledge of the Spirit.

The Sufis believe that God had to look into the face of the non-being (Asat, split as A – Sat, meaning that which is not true, that which has no substance) in order to see and realize the infinite variety of beauty and the true essence common to all that beauty. The non-being, the creatures, and Praktri (nature) are only a reflection, a mirror image of God, and therefore, only A – Sat, that which does not actually exist, and hence, not true. The actual truth is hidden within God (Brahman).

In human terms, this is hard to understand. It becomes easy to comprehend if we use the mirror analogy once more. If we see our reflection in the mirror momentarily, we know we see ourselves. But are we really there in the mirror? No. In that moment, however, we felt our own reality or existence as opposed to our reflection. Our existence at that point outside the mirror is the actual truth. But how can we be the Truth outside the mirror and not the Truth inside the mirror? Because, the image in the mirror is but a reflection, just like we are a reflection when viewed from Brahman's point. Just like our reflection in the mirror is there only as long as we stand in front of it and perceive it, so it is when Brahman sees us in the mirror of His mind's eye. We are but a reflection in His mirror as long as He perceives us.

How do we become and perceive the Truth then? When it is said that we are only a reflection of the True Brahman, it means we have to realize and accept two things:

1. We came into being for Brahman.
2. We are indeed Brahman.

Then only the Truth remains, for if we are indeed Brahman, then we are also seeing our own reflection. So, the Creator and the created both perceive the reflection in the mirror as just that.

'Sat' has to become 'Asat' in order to realize its true nature. There has to be an opposite, a contrast for truth to register. If there were no bad, only good, then we would not know 'good' as good. It would simply exist without any essence, any definition. Existence without essence is useless. And essence is always followed by existence. If 'Tat' is essence, then 'Sat' is existence, the Complete Being. It is the substance of the universe, and this substance is good and pure. Therefore, it is par excellence.

Those who seek spiritual austerity, says the Bhagwad Gita, start with Om, the unspoken first word. Then they go on to offer sacrifices and observe austerities by associating with That Supreme Essence, surrendering to 'That'. This surrendering and sacrificing to 'That' with goodness and purity in heart is the highest excellence and enables the non-being to realize the Truth.

What is this Truth?

1. Brahman or OM is the life of all life.
2. Brahman or OM is the cause of all causes.
3. Brahman or OM is the sustainer of everything.
4. Brahman or OM is the experience and the one who experiences everything.

This four-fold truth Lord Krishna declares forcefully in the Bhagwad Gita (7. 6-7):

Aham kritsnasya jagataha prabhavaha pralayastatha
Mattaha parataram na anyet kinchit asti Dhananjaya
Mayi sarvamidam protam sutre manigana iva.
"I am the birth of the cosmos: its dissolution also (too)
I am He who causes, No other beside Me.
Upon Me, these worlds are held
Like pearls strung on a thread." And in 13:22
Upadrishta anumanta cha bharta bhokta Maheshwaraha

"The Supreme Brahman in this body, also known as the witness

Approves, supports (sustains) and sanctions all actions, experiencing all our experiences."

The realization that One Principle runs through all things in the universe is 'Gyan' (knowledge). The realization that That One Principle is responsible for causing the universe is 'Vigyan' (literally meaning science. In depth meaning: scientific philosophical knowledge, wisdom). In Vigyan is contained Gyan, and that is the truth.

OM Tat Sat

SINGULARITY

OM is Singularity. How and why? The heat in the sun, the force in lightning, the chemicals in gases, the position and staying power of stars and planets – all these are core things held together by one thing and one thing only, and that is OM. OM not only vibrates through the cosmos as sound, space, wind, energy, light, water and earth, but is sound, space, wind, energy, light, water and earth, and so is Singularity. OM is the hum that connects the universe. OM is that which binds together, pulls together, holds together everything in the universe. Even though entropy may be present, it is controlled by this Singularity, which has unlimited staying power and reigning power. It is the ultimate source of energy (Shakti). It is Radiant Energy.

While It has the power of everything in the universe, everything in the universe does not have its power. It is the power in everything. Even though It has the energy and light of everything in the universe, and lights and energizes everything in the universe, Its Radiant power does not destroy once you come in its presence, i.e., get to know It. On the contrary, it radiates with the energy of millions of suns, and yet, enfolds you in blissful warmth.

OM can be heard because of **sound**, which can be heard because of **air**, which is there because of **space**, which is seen because of **light**, which is caused by **energy**, the heat in which releases the **water**, from which rises the manifested **Earth**, which engulfs **life**, which makes you aware of **elements (senses)**, enjoyment of which is limited by **time**, which forces the impression of **timelessness (immortality)**, the spirit of which is **Revelation**, where everything merges (reverts back) into **One**, which is **Singularity - OM.**